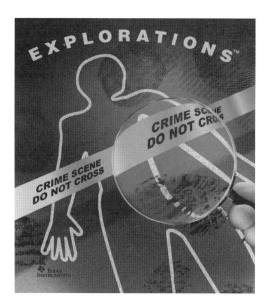

Forensics:
Connecting Science Investigations with TI Data Collection Activities

Jackie Bonneau

Important notice regarding book materials

Texas Instruments Incorporated
7800 Banner Drive, MS 3918
Dallas, Texas 75251
Attention: Manager, Business Services

Printed in the United States of America.

ISBN: 1-886309-73-6

CBL 2, CBR 2, and TI Connect are trademarks of Texas Instruments Incorporated.
Vernier EasyLink and Vernier EasyData are trademarks of Vernier Software & Technology.
All other trademarks are the property of their respective owners.

We invite your comments and suggestions about this book. Call us at 1-800-TI-CARES or send e-mail to ti-cares@ti.com. You can also call or send e-mail to request information about other current and future publications from Texas Instruments.

Visit the TI World Wide Web home page. The web address is: education.ti.com

Table of Contents

Case Number and Title	Learning Objectives	Materials (per group unless otherwise noted)
Case File 1 Tracks of a Killer: Using footprints to estimate height	• determine if there is a relationship between the length of a person's stride and his or her height • determine if there is a relationship between the size of a person's shoes and his or her height • efficiently gather data to test for correlations between height, shoe size, and stride length • use a linear regression model of the data to predict height based on stride length	• TI-83/TI-84 Plus™ Family • metric tape measure or meterstick • metric ruler • straight walkway at least 10 m long • chalk or tape
Case File 2 Bouncing Back: Using ground-penetrating radar to locate buried objects	• explore the use of ground-penetrating radar (GPR) to find buried materials • detect the presence of an object, using a range finder • distinguish between different-shaped objects, using a range finder	• TI-83/TI-84 Plus™ Family Vernier EasyData™ application • Calculator-Based Ranger 2™ (CBR 2™) • small box or block of wood • several large boxes, each containing an unknown object
Case File 3 Name That Tune: Matching musical tones through waveform analysis	• identify the musical notes that make up the combination to a safe • detect the waveform of a musical note, using a Microphone • calculate the frequency of a musical note from the period of its waveform	• TI-83/TI-84 Plus™ Family Calculator-Based Laboratory 2™ (CBL 2™) and link cable • Vernier EasyData™ application • Vernier Microphone™ • 6 tuning forks of different frequencies • soft tuning-fork hammer
Case File 4 Flipping Coins: Density as a characteristic property	• identify counterfeit coins based on the characteristic property of density • model data using a linear equation • interpret the slope and intercept values from a linear model • identify a characteristic property of a substance	• TI-83/TI-84 Plus™ Family Vernier EasyData™ application • Vernier EasyLink™ • Dual-Range Force Sensor • clamp or heavy tape • light plastic coffee cup • string • 20 pennies dated 1963–1981 • 20 pennies dated 1982 • 20 pennies dated after 1982

Case Number and Title	Learning Objectives	Materials (per group unless otherwise noted)
Case File 5 The Ink Is Still Wet: Using colorimetry to identify an unknown ink	• identify an unknown ink by its light absorbance characteristics • measure a solution's absorbance of different colors (wavelengths) of light	• TI-83/TI-84 Plus™ Family • Vernier EasyLink™ • Vernier EasyData™ application • Colorimeter • 6 cuvettes • colored wax pencil • 5 dropper bottles, with 10 mL samples of 5 different diluted black inks • 1 dropper bottle with 10 mL of diluted unknown black ink • deionized or distilled water • lint-free tissues • goggles (1 pair per student)
Case File 6 Measuring Momentum: Using momentum to determine intent	• establish a relationship between the momentum of a vehicle and the distance a stationary object moves when the vehicle hits it • accurately gather data from a collision of a vehicle with a stationary object • establish a relationship between the distance an object moves after a collision with a vehicle and the momentum of the vehicle	• TI-83/TI-84 Plus™ Family • Vernier EasyData™ application • Vernier EasyLink™ • Dual-Range Force Sensor • Calculator-Based Ranger 2™ (CBR 2™) • clamp or heavy tape • 1.5 m (or longer) ramp of strong cardboard or wood • meterstick • 25 cm (or higher) support for ramp • masking tape • 450–500 g vehicle about 7 cm tall • book, 5–7 cm thick • book, 2 cm thick • thread or wide rubber band
Case File 7: Drug Tests: Identifying an unknown chemical	• identify an unknown powder using physical and chemical properties • distinguish between physical and chemical properties • distinguish between qualitative and quantitative observation	• TI-83/TI-84 Plus™ Family • Vernier EasyData™ application • Vernier EasyLink™ • pH Sensor • Conductivity Probe • vinegar • 5 known and 1 unknown "drug" samples (4 g of each) • distilled or deionized water • spoons and/or weighing paper (one per sample) • filter paper • six 50 mL beakers • stirring rod • disposable pipettes or droppers • wash bottle (with deionized water) • magnifying glass • balance • lint-free tissues • goggles (1 pair per student)

Case Number and Title	Learning Objectives	Materials (per group unless otherwise noted)
Case File 8: No Dumping: Using soil characteristics to link suspects to a crime scene	• identify characteristics of different soils to demonstrate that a suspect has been at a scene • use characteristic properties to identify a sample • measure the pH of soils • measure the water absorbency of soils • measure the conductivity of soils	• TI-83/TI-84 Plus™ Family • Vernier EasyData™ application • Vernier EasyLink™ • pH Sensor • Conductivity Probe • magnifying glass • coarse filter papers (12.5 cm diameter) • distilled or deionized water • lint-free tissues • wash bottle (with deionized water) • 100 mL graduated cylinder • five 250 mL beakers • 5 spoons or weighing papers • 400 mL beaker • 50 mL beaker for deionized water • stirring rod • funnel large enough for 50 g of soil and 100 mL of water • balance • 100 g each of soil samples for 4 suspects and 1 crime scene • goggles (1 pair per student)
Case File 9: Killer Cup of Coffee: Using colorimetry to determine concentration of a poison	• use Beer's law to determine the concentration of iron(III)thiocyanate ($FeSCN^{2+}$) in an unknown solution • use colorimetry to determine the concentration of a colored species in a solution • use a linear relationship to model Beer's law • learn the importance of carefully prepared standards	• TI-83/TI-84 Plus™ Family • Vernier EasyData™ application • Vernier EasyLink™ • Colorimeter • 7 cuvettes • colored wax pencil • distilled or deionized water • 50 mL of 0.15 M stock $FeSCN^{2+}$ solution • 5 mL of $FeSCN^{2+}$ solution with unknown concentration • two 10 mL pipettes or graduated cylinders • two 50 mL beakers • 5 stirring rods • 2 droppers • 5 test tubes • test-tube rack • lint-free tissues • waste beaker • goggles (1 pair per student)
Case File 10: Dropped at the Scene: Blood spatter analysis	• determine the height of a source of blood spatters or drops • graph data to find quantitative relationships • create a standard reference curve for comparison with unknown data	• TI-83/TI-84 Plus™ Family • newspaper • 13 pieces of white paper • disposable pipettes or droppers • simulated blood • calipers, or compass and metric ruler • meterstick

Case Number and Title	Learning Objectives	Materials (per group unless otherwise noted)
Case File 11: Ashes to Ashes: Using evaporation rate to identify an unknown liquid	• identify the likely accelerant in an arson • identify a solution, based on evaporation rate • understand that evaporation rate is a characteristic property of a liquid	• TI-83/TI-84 Plus™ Family • Vernier EasyTemp™ temperature probe • Vernier EasyData™ application • accelerant samples from 4 suspects • accelerant sample from crime scene • 5 small test tubes • test-tube rack • 6 pieces of filter paper cut into 2 × 2 cm squares • 6 small rubber bands • lint-free tissues or paper towels • goggles (1 pair per student)
Case File 12: Hit and Run: Using information from an event data recorder to reconstruct an accident	• simulate the use of an event data recorder (EDR) in order to show how the evidence gathered by this device can be used for legal purposes • show how accident scenes can be recreated through an analysis of the data that are gathered by an EDR • learn how distance traveled, velocity, and acceleration are related to one another • learn how the appearance of an acceleration, velocity, or distance vs. time graph can be used to predict the appearance of the other graphs	• TI-83/TI-84 Plus™ Family • Vernier EasyData™ application • Calculator-Based Ranger 2™ (CBR 2™) • toy car, at least 5 cm tall
Case File 13: Life in the Fast Lane: Using skid marks to determine vehicle speed	• determine the speed of a vehicle before its brakes were applied • determine the coefficient of friction between a vehicle and a road surface • convert between SI units and Imperial units • rearrange equations to solve for different variables	• TI-83/TI-84 Plus™ Family • Vernier EasyData™ application • Vernier EasyLink™ • Dual-Range Force Sensor • Hall's carriage or heavy toy car • thread, string, or yarn • rubber bands (for a Hall's carriage) or tissue (for a toy car) • meterstick or metric tape measure • C-clamp or duct tape • chalk or tape • flat, smooth surface (floor or table)
Case File 14: Hot Air, Cold Body: Using Newton's law of cooling to determine time of death	• determine the time of death of a person who has died within the last few hours • create a temperature vs. time graph for cooling • use the cooling-rate equation to estimate time of death • become familiar with Newton's law of cooling	• TI-83/TI-84 Plus™ Family • Vernier EasyTemp temperature probe • Vernier EasyData™ application • ring stand with clamp • model victim

Note to the Teacher

The science of forensics has become increasingly popular in secondary education because it encompasses aspects of mathematics, physics, chemistry, biology, and even geology. The high level of student interest in forensics activities also makes them ideal for introducing students to real-world applications of science and mathematics. Forensic science provides a perfect answer to the age-old question, "When am I ever going to need to know this stuff?"

About This Book

This book has been designed for teachers at the high school level who wish to introduce their students to forensics, using engaging and realistic laboratory activities. The book contains 14 lab activities dealing with various aspects of forensic science. The activities span a wide range of subject matter and conceptual difficulty. They are arranged in order of the increasing complexity of the calculator skills required. Most activities suggest ways to increase or decrease difficulty or teaching time.

Each lab is preceded by a short scenario that introduces the concepts or methods to be addressed in the lab. These introductory sequences are designed to "hook" the students and show them situations that require various forensic techniques. The Case Analysis questions for each activity relate to the concepts and techniques addressed in the lab, and many require the students to "solve" the crime introduced in the scenario with the data they collect.

Tips and Resources

Appendix A contains tips on basic calculator use. A reference guide for using the Vernier EasyData application can be found in **Appendix B**. If students are unfamiliar with the calculator or have not used it for a while, you may wish to photocopy some or all of these tips and give them to the students for reference while they are conducting the lab activities. **Appendix C** contains a list of materials needed to complete all activities in the book.

Because every class is different, it is important to test each lab yourself before assigning it to your students. In addition, many of the activities require you to generate "evidence" for your students to analyze during the course of the lab. You should read over each activity carefully to determine whether or not it is appropriate for your needs and those of your students.

Texas Instruments maintains a Web site called the **Activities Exchange** where teachers can share ideas and tips about different activities that utilize the TI family of calculators. Share your activities and lessons, or simply browse for ideas at http://education.ti.com/exchange.

From the CD-ROM

You can **Explore** an Interactive Case Demonstration, **Download** customizable Case File materials, and **Download** the Vernier EasyData™ application.

The CD-ROM includes a folder for each activity in the book. The folders contain the following materials:
- a copy of each lab in Adobe® .pdf format
- a Microsoft® Word .doc file containing the Evidence Record (data collection sheet) and Case Analysis questions for each activity (a file that can be edited, so you can add or remove questions or change the data collection sheet format)

The CD-ROM also includes the latest (as of publication of this book) version of the Vernier EasyData software program. Updates to this application and instructions for downloading or installing the EasyData application can be accessed at http://education.ti.com/apps.

Need Help?

While the calculators and probes are designed for easy use, sometimes unexpected problems do occur. Both Texas Instruments and Vernier provide extensive support for their activities and products.

For questions about, or problems with, calculators and most software applications, contact

Texas Instruments
  http://education.ti.com
  TI-cares@ti.com
  1-800-TI-CARES

For questions about, or problems with, sensors, probes, or the EasyData application, contact

Vernier Software & Technology
  http://www.vernier.com/products.html
  info@vernier.com
  1-888-837-6437

About the Authors & Consultants

Jacklyn Bonneau has taught science for over 31 years and has used scientific probes for data collection since 1982. The last 10 years of her teaching career have been spent at the Massachusetts Academy of Mathematics and Science. Her main teaching concentrations are in chemistry, physics, and research and introduction to engineering design. Jacklyn first became interested in teaching forensics in the late 1990s and has offered one-week institutes on the topic to interested teachers during the summer. She has also coordinated numerous workshops on the local, state, and national level. In these workshops, participants become students and experience the thrill of "finding the answer" for themselves. Jacklyn has been a consultant for Vernier Software and Technology since 1990 and an instructor for T^3 since 1998 and was involved in the development of the Calculator-Based Laboratory™ (CBL™).

Carl Leinbach is a retired professor of mathematics and computer science at Gettysburg College in Gettysburg, Pennsylvania. He has served as a T^3 instructor and has given presentations at T^3 international conferences along with his wife, Pat. He also has served the Mathematical Association of America (MAA) as the chair of the Committee on Computers in Mathematics Education, as the software reviews editor for the journals of the MAA, and as an active member of the Committee on Mini Courses, which selects and coordinates the mini courses given at the joint meetings of the American Mathematical Society and the MAA. In addition to pursuing his mathematical interests, Carl has served as an EMT instructor in Adams County, Pennsylvania, and as an ambulance attendant for the Biglerville Fire Department in Biglerville, Pennsylvania.

Patricia Leinbach served three terms as the coroner of Adams County, Pennsylvania, before taking up her current post as chief deputy coroner of Adams County. As coroner, she conducted over 700 death investigations and served as the president of the Pennsylvania State Coroner's Association. She and her husband, Carl, have addressed the Teachers Teaching with Technology (T^3) International Conference (Dallas, Texas) and the International Technology in Mathematics Conference (Liverpool, UK) with their presentation "Estimating the Time Since Death." Pat has also served as an emergency medical technician (EMT) instructor in Adams County, Pennsylvania, and as ambulance captain for the Biglerville Fire Department in Biglerville, Pennsylvania.

Tracks of a Killer: Using footprints to estimate height

Analyze the relationships between shoe size, stride length, and height, and then use that information to identify the likely killer.

The body of famous pop music producer Jonathan Wallace was found in his bathtub. It is our hypothesis that an intruder surprised the victim and drowned him. The only clue at the crime scene was a set of muddy footprints leading from a nearby window to the bathroom and back again. The footprints were smeared, so their exact size could not be determined. The soles of the shoes had no pattern. It will be difficult to match the footprints to any particular pair of shoes.

Three suspects were questioned immediately following the murder:

Penelope Paige, pop star: 5'4"/green eyes/blond hair
Possible motive: She is suing Wallace over the failure of her last album.
Rex Chapman, rock guitarist: 5'8"/brown eyes/brown hair
Possible motive: He accused Wallace of stealing profits from his hit single "Walk It Off."
Dirty Dawg, rapper: 6'0"/brown eyes/black hair
Possible motive: He wants out of a record contract with Wallace.

Victim Jonathan Wallace. Found 2 p.m. on 10/5/05. Time of death estimated at between 8 and 10 a.m.

Footprints presumed to have been left by the murderer. Prints are 25–30 cm long. Heel-to-heel stride length is 64–65 cm.

Forensics Objectives

- determine if there is a relationship between the length of a person's stride and his or her height
- determine if there is a relationship between the size of a person's shoes and his or her height

Science and Mathematics Objectives

- efficiently gather data to test for correlations between height, shoe size, and stride length
- use a linear regression model of the data to predict height based on stride length

Materials

- TI-83/TI-84 Plus™ Family
- for station 1: metric tape measure or meterstick
- for station 2: metric ruler
- for station 3: metric tape measure or meterstick
      straight walkway at least 10 m long
      chalk or tape

Procedure

Part I: Collecting the Data ● ● ●

1. Set up three stations with two people at each, one person to collect data and one person to record data.

    a) At station 1, use the tape measure or meterstick to measure each person's height without shoes to the nearest half centimeter, and record it in the Evidence Record next to the person's name.

    b) At station 2, have each person remove his or her right shoe. Turn the shoe over and use a ruler to measure the distance from the tip of the toe to the end of the heel. Record the length of the person's shoe in the Evidence Record.

    c) At station 3, mark a starting line with chalk or tape. Have each person stand with the backs of his or her heels at the edge of the starting line. Starting at this point, each person should take 10 normal-length walking steps in a straight line (see the diagram below). After the 10th step, the person should stop and bring his or her heels together. Mark the final position of the back of the person's heels, and measure the distance in centimeters between that mark and the edge of the starting line. Calculate the average stride length by dividing this distance by 10. Record each person's average stride length in centimeters in the Evidence Record .

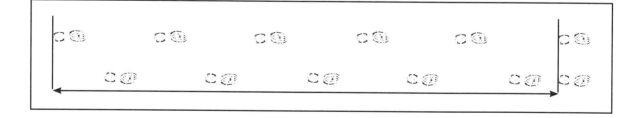

2. When all of the data are collected, compile a complete record for all individuals on a master Evidence Record.

Part II: Analyzing the Data ● ● ●

3. Enter your data in the calculator.

   a) Turn the calculator on.

   b) Press ⟨STAT⟩ ⟨ENTER⟩. This will bring up three lists: L1, L2, and L3. If the lists contain old data, you can clear them by highlighting the list number (use the arrow keys to move around) and then pressing ⟨CLEAR⟩ ⟨ENTER⟩.

   c) Enter each student's height in L1, shoe length in L2, and average stride length in L3. Make sure that all of the data for a particular student are in the same row. Do *not* enter the students' names in the data lists in your calculator.

L1	L2	L3	1
146.5	23	58	
158.5	25.5	70.5	
186.5	28	88	
176.5	23	82	
180	30.5	85	
161	25.5	64.5	
174	28	77.5	

L1(1)=146.5

Use the arrow keys to move between L1, L2, and L3. If you make a mistake typing in the number, highlight the wrong number, press ⟨ENTER⟩, and then key in the correct number. To delete an extra number, press ⟨DEL⟩. This will delete the number and move the entire row up. To insert a number, press ⟨2nd⟩ ⟨DEL⟩ and then the number.

4. Begin analyzing the data by graphing height versus stride length.

   a) Press ⟨2nd⟩ ⟨Y=⟩. This will take you to the **STAT PLOT** screen.

   b) Choose **PLOT1** by pressing ⟨ENTER⟩.

   c) In the resulting screen, use the arrow keys to highlight **On** and press ⟨ENTER⟩. Use the arrow keys to move down to **Type**. Choose a dot (scatter) plot by highlighting the first of the pictured graphs and pressing ⟨ENTER⟩.

   d) To put the height data on the *x*-axis, move down to **Xlist**. Choose **L1** by pressing ⟨2nd⟩ ⟨1⟩.

   e) To put stride length on the *y*-axis, move down to **YList**. Choose **L3** by pressing ⟨2nd⟩ ⟨3⟩.

   f) To mark each data point with a box, move down to **Mark**, use the arrow keys to highlight the box, and press ⟨ENTER⟩.

   g) To set the graph scaling values, press ⟨ZOOM⟩.

   h) Choose option **9: ZoomStat** to scale the axes of the graph to show your data correctly. Your screen should now change to show a graph of your data.

To select a menu item, either press the number corresponding to that item *or* use the arrow keys to highlight the item and press ⟨ENTER⟩.

The picture below shows a graph of some sample data. (Don't expect your data to look exactly like this!)

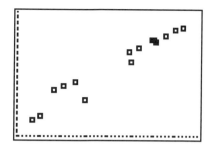

Next, you will use the calculator to determine the equation for the straight line that fits your data the best. It is important to have an equation that describes the relationship between height and stride length. If you have an equation, you can predict the height of *any* person based on the length of the person's stride.

There is a specific kind of mathematical formula that can be used to determine the equation for a straight line that best fits a group of data points. It is called a *linear regression*. In order to use this formula, we have to assume that the relationship between height and stride length is linear. In other words, we have to assume that height and stride length are related by an equation that is in the following form:

$$\text{stride length} = (a)(\text{height}) + b$$

where the a and b are constants. It is possible to calculate the equation by hand, but it takes a long time and is a little bit tedious. However, your calculator has a program called LinReg that will calculate the a and b for your data quickly.

5. Before using the calculator's LinReg program to calculate the linear regression, turn on the calculator's **Diagnostic** function. This will tell the calculator to calculate how well the line fits the data, in addition to calculating the a and b values.
    a)   Go to the calculator's function catalog by pressing ⟨2nd⟩ ⟨0⟩.
    b)   Use the arrow keys to scroll down until the **DiagnosticOn** option is highlighted, and then press ⟨ENTER⟩ ⟨ENTER⟩. Your screen should look like this:

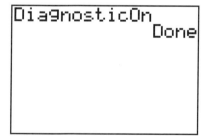

6. Use the LinReg function to perform the linear regression and store the resulting equation in variable Y1.
    a)   Press ⟨STAT⟩, highlight **CALC**, and choose option **4: LinReg(ax + b)**. This will print **LinReg(ax + b)** on the Home screen.
    b)   You need to tell the calculator where your data are and where to store the final equation. You want to find the line that describes the relationship between height (list L1) and stride length (list L3). Press ⟨2nd⟩ ⟨1⟩ ⟨,⟩ ⟨2nd⟩ ⟨3⟩ ⟨,⟩ to tell the calculator that lists L1 and L3 contain the data that you want to fit a line to.
    c)   To indicate that you want to store the equation in variable Y1, press ⟨VARS⟩ ⟨▷⟩ to select **Y-VARS**. Press ⟨ENTER⟩ ⟨ENTER⟩ to tell the calculator to store the equation in the Y1 variable. The Main screen should now show this: **LinReg(ax+b) L1,L3,Y1**.

d) Press ⏎ENTER⏎ to execute the LinReg function. This calculates the equation for the straight line that fits through your data best. The screen will display the a and b values that make the linear equation fit the data. The r^2 value tells you how well the line fits the data. An r^2 value that is close to 1 means that the line fits the data very well. The picture below shows the equation for the line that fits the sample data.

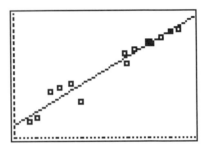

Write the r^2 value that the calculator computed for your data into your Evidence Record. Also record the equation describing the data that the calculator computed.

e) The equation that describes the data is stored in the variable Y1. You can see this equation by pressing ⟨Y=⟩.

f) Press ⟨GRAPH⟩ to see how well a straight line fits your data points. The picture below shows the straight line that best fits the sample data.

It might take a few seconds for the regression line to show up on your screen. If you pressed ⟨GRAPH⟩ and only your points are showing, look in the upper right corner of the screen. There probably will be a small moving line there. When that line is moving, it indicates that the calculator is "thinking." When the line goes away, the calculator has finished doing its computations.

7. Now determine whether or not there is a relationship between height and shoe size. Repeat steps 4–6, but make the following changes:
   a) In step 4c, use the arrow keys and ⟨ENTER⟩ to turn Plot 1 off.
   b) Use the arrow keys to select Plot 2 and turn it on.
   c) For Plot 2, make sure height is on the x-axis by setting **XList** to **L1** (press ⟨2nd⟩ ⟨1⟩).
   d) Put shoe size on the y-axis by setting the **YList** to **L2** (press ⟨2nd⟩ ⟨2⟩).
   e) In step 6b, complete LinReg(ax + b) by typing ⟨2nd⟩ ⟨1⟩ ⟨,⟩ ⟨2nd⟩ ⟨2⟩ ⟨,⟩ ⟨VARS⟩ ⟨▷⟩ ⟨ENTER⟩ ⟨▼⟩ ⟨ENTER⟩. The screen should read **LinReg(ax+b) L1,L2,Y2**. The equation for the line describing these data is stored in variable Y2. Write down the equation describing the data, as well as the r^2 value for this line, in your Evidence Record.

8. Answer the questions in the Case Analysis, using your results. Remember that the equation describing the relationship between height and stride length is stored in variable Y1, and the equation describing height and shoe size is in variable Y2. To see these equations, press ⟨Y=⟩. If you forgot to write down one of the r^2 values, repeat steps 7a–7c with the appropriate inputs to the equation. This will print the r^2 value on the screen again.

Remember that you can get back to the Home screen by pressing ⟨2nd⟩ ⟨MODE⟩.

NAME: _____

DATE: _____

Evidence Record

Student Name	Height (cm) (L1)	Shoe Length (cm) (L2)	Stride Length (cm) (L3)

r^2 value for height versus stride length: _____

Equation describing the relationship between height and stride length:

_____

r^2 value for height versus shoe size: _____

Equation describing the relationship between height and shoe size:

_____

Case Analysis

1. Based on your data, is there a linear relationship between height and stride length?
2. What is the value of r^2 for the straight line that best describes your data for height versus stride length? Do you think the straight line fits these data well?
3. Based on your data, is there a linear relationship between height and shoe size?
4. Do you think that it is possible to infer a person's height from his or her shoe size? Explain your answer.
5. Using the relationship between height and stride length that you calculated, determine the approximate heights of people with the following stride lengths: a) 75.5 cm, b) 45.5 cm, and c) 50.0 cm.
6. Using the relationship between height and stride length that you calculated, predict the stride length of a person who is not a student in your class (for example, your teacher, your principal, or a student in a different class) based on his or her height. Then measure the person's actual stride length. How close was your prediction to the actual stride length?
7. Suppose you measure the stride length of a set of footprints, you predict that the person who made the footprints is 175 cm tall, and you later find out that the person who made the footprints is actually only 152 cm tall. Give one possible reason that your prediction was incorrect.
8. Using the relationships that you calculated, determine which of the three suspects most likely left the footprints to and from Jonathan Wallace's bathroom. Show all your calculations. (Hint: In the equation that you wrote down, *x* is stride length and *y* is height.)

Case File 1
Tracks of a Killer: Using footprints to estimate height

Teacher Notes

Teaching time: one class period

This lab introduces the concepts of linear regression and r^2 values through an analysis of the relationship between stride length, shoe size, and height.

Tips

- Having three stations may not work well with some classes because the students will spend some time waiting for others to have measurements taken. You may want to break up the class into groups of three or four students; each group will make all three measurements.
- Make a transparency of the Evidence Record table to be used as a master Evidence Record. Students can record their individual data on the transparency, and then they can all copy the compiled data into their own Evidence Records.

Modifications

If time is short or students are less advanced, steps 1b and 7, as well as Case Analysis questions 3 and 4, can be eliminated.

Sample Data

Student Name	Height (cm) (L1)	Shoe Length (cm) (L2)	Stride Length (cm) (L3)
Student 1	146.5	23.0	58.0
Student 2	158.5	25.5	70.5
Student 3	186.5	28.0	88.0
Student 4	176.5	23.0	82.0
Student 5	180.0	30.5	85.0
Student 6	161.0	25.5	64.5
Student 7	174.0	28.0	77.5
Student 8	189.0	28.5	89.0
Student 9	181.5	23.5	84.5
Student 10	184.0	30.0	86.5
Student 11	149.0	23.0	59.5
Student 12	152.5	24.0	68.0
Student 13	155.5	26.0	69.5
Student 14	173.5	24.5	81.0
Student 15	181.0	30.0	85.0

r^2 value for height versus stride length: **0.948**
Equation describing the relationship between height and stride length:
     $y = 0.7098x - 44.05$

r^2 value for height versus shoe size: **0.409**
Equation describing the relationship between height and shoe size:
     $y = 0.1206x + 5.703$

Case Analysis Answers

1. Based on your data, is there a linear relationship between height and stride length?
   There should be a clear linear relationship between height and stride length. The data points should fall on a fairly straight line.
2. What is the value of r^2 for the straight line that best describes your data for height versus stride length? Do you think the straight line fits these data well?
   The r^2 values should be fairly close to 1 (0.95 or 0.90 is acceptable). If the values are significantly lower than this, it is possible that the students entered incorrect data or that their measurements were inaccurate.
3. Based on your data, is there a linear relationship between height and shoe size?
   There should not be a clearly linear relationship between height and shoe size.
4. Do you think that it is possible to infer a person's height from his or her shoe size? Explain your answer.
   No, it is generally not possible to predict a person's height from his or her shoe size.
5. Using the relationship between height and stride length that you calculated, determine the approximate heights of people with the following stride lengths: a) 75.5 cm, b) 45.5 cm, and c) 50.0 cm.
   Answers will vary depending on calculated height–stride-length equations.
6. Using the relationship between height and stride length that you calculated, predict the stride length of a person who is not a student in your class (for example, your teacher, your principal, or a student in a different class) based on his or her height. Then measure the person's actual stride length. How close was your prediction to the actual stride length?
   Answers will vary.
7. Suppose you measure the stride length of a set of footprints, you predict that the person who made the footprints is 175 cm tall, and you later find out that the person who made the footprints is actually only 152 cm tall. Give one possible reason that your prediction was incorrect.
   Possible reasons for incorrect predictions of height include the following: the person was running or was taking larger or smaller steps than usual, the person's normal stride does not follow the usual trend, and the stride length was measured incorrectly.
8. Using the relationships that you calculated, determine which of the three suspects most likely left the footprints to and from Jonathan Wallace's bathroom. Show all your calculations. (Hint: In the equation that you wrote down, x is stride length and y is height.)
   Answers will vary; based on the sample data here, Penelope Paige most likely left the footprints (her height is closest to the calculated height of 5 ft).

$$\text{stride length} = 0.7098 \, (\text{height}) - 44.05$$

$$\text{height} = \frac{\text{stride length} + 44.05}{0.7098} = \frac{64.5 + 44.05}{0.7098}$$

$$= 152.9 \text{ cm} = 60 \text{ in}$$

Case File 2

Bouncing Back: Using ground-penetrating radar to locate buried objects

Locate Mrs. Holloway's car and help solve this cold case.

To: Detective Sergeant Ashanti
Re: Possible new evidence in Holloway case

We have just received new information on this unsolved, high-profile case from several years ago. On May 6, 2000, the wife of billionaire oil tycoon Donald Holloway drove away in her car and never returned. As we never found any evidence of foul play, we believed that Mrs. Holloway left her husband and changed her identity. Recently, Mrs. Holloway's California vanity license plate, OIL GIRL, was found outside a remote gas station along the Desert Highway. This particular gas station happens to be quite close to lands owned by the Holloway oil empire. Also uncovered in recent weeks have been several documents detailing the purchase of some large properties along the road. It now looks like Holloway may have killed his wife and buried her and her car at one of the properties. Sample email is attached.

From: jwinchester@ ZongoReelEstayt.com
Date: May 8, 2000
To: dholloway@hollowayoil.com
Subject: RE: your needs

Mr. Holloway –

Per your request, I have identified four abandoned sites along Desert Highway that would suit your needs. The following locations are very remote and have been untouched for years:

» the old Two Tree golf course
» the 1960s government rocket-testing site (now deserted)
» the construction site on 31st and Desert
» the abandoned Bright Days housing development

Good luck with your latest endeavor.

Forensics Objective

- explore the use of ground-penetrating radar (GPR) to find buried materials

Science and Mathematics Objectives

- detect the presence of an object, using a range finder
- distinguish between different-shaped objects, using a range finder

Materials (for each group)

- TI-83/TI-84 Plus™ Family
- Vernier EasyData™ application
- Calculator-Based Ranger 2™ (CBR 2™)
- USB cable
- small box or block of wood
- several large boxes, each containing an unknown object

Procedure

1. Attach the USB cable to the CBR 2. Connect the other end of the cable to the calculator's USB port. The EasyData App should self-load. If it does not, press ⟨APPS⟩ and select **: EasyData**.

2. Set up the CBR 2 to collect one data point every 0.05 seconds for 200 seconds.
   a) Select ⟨Setup⟩. Select option **2: Time Graph**.
   b) Select ⟨Edit⟩ to change the experiment parameters.
   c) Press ⟨CLEAR⟩ and type **0.05** for the time between samples.
   d) Select ⟨Next⟩, press ⟨CLEAR⟩, and type **200** for the number of samples.
   e) Select ⟨Next⟩. Confirm that the experiment parameters are correct (sample interval = 0.05 seconds, number of samples = 200, experiment length = 10 seconds), and then select ⟨OK⟩.

3. Get to know how the CBR 2 displays its data.
   a) Place a block of wood or a small box on your desk. Make sure that there is nothing else on the surface of your desk.
   b) Hold the CBR 2 about a meter above your desktop and toward one end of your desk. Select ⟨Start⟩. You will hear a rapid clicking sound from the detector. Slowly move the motion detector, at a constant height above the desktop, from one end of your desk to the other end. Make sure that the light-gray part of the detector is facing the desk and that it passes over the top of the block or box on your desk.
   c) After 10 seconds, the clicking will stop. The screen will say that data are being transferred. Then you should see a display like the one shown below. (Note: It may take a few seconds for the data to transfer. Be patient!)

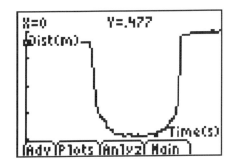

---

d) Your display will look like the one shown above only if you have moved the detector slowly, at constant speed, and at a constant height. If you turn your calculator upside down, the image looks more like something sitting on the desktop.

e) Using the arrow keys, you can see how far the desktop and the top of the box were from the CBR 2. (Note: If you do not get a graph like the one on the previous page, repeat step 3b. Make sure that your desk is clear, that the light-gray part of the detector is facing the desk, and that you maintain a constant speed and height above the desk.

f) Select (Main) to return to the Main screen. Repeat steps 3a–d with the box in a different orientation, such as on one of its ends. If you get a message about overwriting stored data runs, select (OK). Explore the graphs until you are comfortable with how the graph shows the location and shape of the object on your desk.

4. Your teacher will direct your group to move to one of the suspected "burial sites" for the car. Record the location of the site in the Evidence Record.

5. Without looking inside the box, probe each of the suspected burial sites.
   a) Rest the CBR 2 on the top edge of a flap that runs the length of the box, with the light-gray part of the detector facing the bottom of the box.
   b) Practice slowly moving the CBR 2 along the flap at a constant height. You need to move the CBR 2 at a speed that will let you move from one end of the box to the other in about 10 seconds. Practice this until you can move the detector at the correct speed and at a constant height.
   c) When you are ready, select (Start). If you get a message about overwriting stored data runs, select (OK). Begin moving the detector just after you begin to hear the rapid clicking noise.
   d) Once the data are transferred, examine the shape of the graph.
   e) Repeat step 5c to see if you get a similar shape again. If not, repeat step 5c until you get a consistent shape. If you are having trouble, ask your teacher for assistance.
   f) Sketch the display shown on the screen into the Evidence Record.

NAME: _____

DATE: _____

Evidence Record

Site Probed by Detector	Sketch of Shape Found by Detector

Case Analysis

1. Analyze the sketches that you have made. Which site contains the buried car? Explain your reasoning.
2. Using the screen captures shown below, determine the height of the object. The **X=** is the time in seconds, and the **Y=** is the distance from the CBR 2 in meters. The cursor location is indicated by an arrow. The **X=** and **Y=** values are shown for the cursor location.

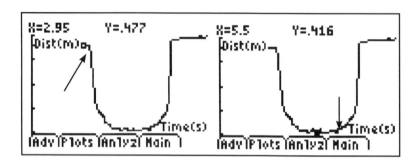

3. Why is it important to move the CBR 2 slowly but at a constant speed? What would happen if you didn't move it at a constant speed?
4. What can make the CBR 2 image (or a real GPR image) of an object look different from the actual profile of the object?
5. How could someone get a more complete image of the object if they used real GPR?

Case File 2
Bouncing Back: Using ground-penetrating radar to locate buried objects

Teacher Notes

Teaching time: one class period

This lab uses the CBR 2™ to determine the presence and height of an object that can't be seen.

Tips

*   Office supply stores sell large boxes. Grocery stores may have some large boxes set out for customers.
*   It may prove easier for students to move the CBR 2 smoothly if it is attached to a meterstick.
*   If you have access to a *very* large box, you can have the students make several passes over the box with the CBR 2, placing the sensor farther from the edge of the box for each pass. In this way, students can produce a slightly more detailed picture of the bottom of the box. They will also simulate the use of GPR more accurately. However, please note that the CBR 2 transmits and receives signals in a cone of about 8°, so only a *very* large box will work.
*   If students are unable to resist the temptation to look inside the boxes, divide the students into groups. Have each group image the object in one of the boxes, and then have the groups trade calculators so that they each have to interpret the display for an object that they did not see.
*   If students are having a hard time interpreting the shapes of the various objects, they can repeat step 3 with several different-shaped objects to become more familiar with the way the calculator displays its data.

Lab Preparation

*   Obtain at least four large boxes (24 × 12 × 14 in, or higher than 14 in). For each box, tape the top flaps up so that they make the box taller. Students should not be able to see what is inside the box when it is placed on a table. (Hint: The top edge of a flap can be used as a guide for the students to rest the CBR 2 on. This will help to keep the CBR 2 at a constant height as the detector is moved from one end of the box to the other. Placing a long strip of cellophane tape on the edge will help the student to move the detector smoothly.)
*   Place an object with a distinctive shape (such as a box, block of wood, large eraser, stapler, roll of tape, or mug) inside each of three boxes. Inside the fourth box, place a model car.

You can make a car from blocks of wood. The motion detector works best on objects with flat surfaces. Make sure that the hood and trunk are at least 3 cm shorter than the top of the car.

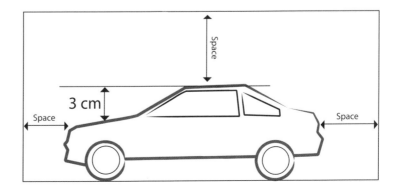

- If you are using a box that is 24 in long, the car should be no more than 20 cm long. If the bottom of the box cannot be detected on both sides of the car, the students will not get a good image of the car.
- Label the boxes with the four suspected burial sites for the car. You may elect to place the boxes at different locations in the room and have student groups go there to collect their data with the CBR 2.
- Students will need to practice on a small block of wood or box to learn how the motion detector displays shapes.
- You may want to leave one of the boxes empty.

Background Information

Ground-penetrating radar (GPR) is a technique that is used frequently by geologists and archaeologists to locate objects and features below the ground. It has also become common to use GPR in forensic investigations. GPR utilizes the same principles as other kinds of radar. Pulses of electromagnetic radiation (often in the frequency range of radio waves) are sent into the ground. These pulses tend to reflect off interfaces in the subsurface—places where two distinctive materials (such as dirt and oil, or rock and water, or soil and metal) meet. The reflected rays travel back to the GPR device, which records the time it takes for the waves to reflect back and the intensity with which they are reflected. With some computer processing, it is possible to create an approximate image of subsurface structures.

Although GPR is a powerful tool, it does have some limitations. The waves tend to attenuate rapidly in water, making it difficult to accurately image saturated soils. The detectors also pick up reflections from surface and near-surface materials, such as trees. Good filtering can remove these "ghost" images, but in general, GPR is best at imaging objects that are 50 cm to 1.5 m in depth. As with all types of radar and sonar, there is a trade-off between resolution and penetration: One can detect deep large objects or shallow small objects but not small objects that are very deep.

Resources

http://www.du.edu/~lconyers/SERDP/GPR2.htm
This Web site provides an in-depth look at how GPR can be used in archaeology. It also contains some basic theory and methodology for GPR.

Sample Data

The shapes the students obtain depend on the objects they are investigating. Below is an example of what a car may look like on the CBR 2 screen.

Site Probed by Detector	Sketch of Shape Found by Detector
(Burial site containing a car)	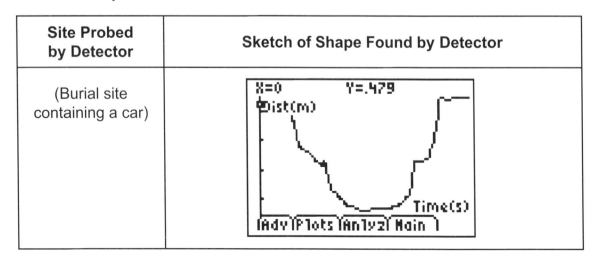

© 2005 TEXAS INSTRUMENTS INCORPORATED

Case Analysis Answers

1. Analyze the sketches that you have made. Which site contains the buried car? Explain your reasoning.

   Student should explain that the shape of the car is different from the other shapes observed; it has contours similar to those of a car.

2. Using the screen captures shown below, determine the height of the object. The **X=** is the time in seconds, and the **Y=** is the distance from the CBR 2 in meters. The cursor location is indicated by an arrow. The **X=** and **Y=** values are shown for the cursor location.

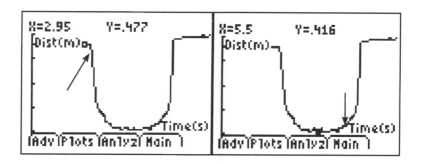

   The height of the object is 0.061 m, or 6.1 cm.

3. Why is it important to move the CBR 2 slowly but at a constant speed? What would happen if you didn't move it at a constant speed?

   It is important to move the CBR 2 at constant speed so that time can be used as an estimate of distance or location. If you change the speed of the CBR 2, the horizontal profile will be out of proportion.

4. What can make the CBR 2 image (or a real GPR image) of an object look different from the actual profile of the object?

   The CBR 2 image won't match the profile of the object if the CBR isn't held at a steady height and moved at a steady speed. Also, the CBR can pick up only the top surface of the object. If an object is complex, many parts of its profile will not be picked up. In addition, other objects between the intended object and the sensor will interfere with the profile of the intended object.

5. How can someone using a real GPR get a more complete image of the object?

   Making many different transects and then piecing those transects together makes a three-dimensional image.

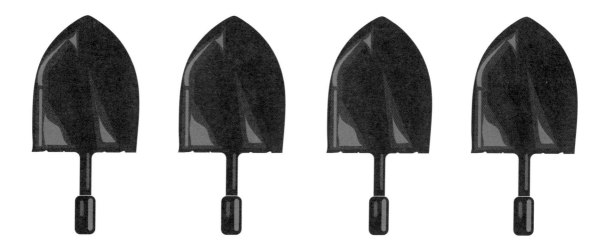

Name That Tune: Matching musical tones through waveform analysis

Identify musical notes based on their frequencies.

Capt. Ramirez:

On Tuesday night, wealthy recluse Tajia Winslow was robbed of her famous collection of rubies, known around the world as the Winslow Ten. The rubies were stored in a safe behind a painting in Ms. Winslow's basement. The safe has a computer lock similar to a telephone keypad. Each time a number on the pad is pushed, a specific tone sounds. This method was developed to assist Ms. Winslow in opening the safe, because she is elderly and has difficulty reading the numbers on the keypad. She thought she was the only person who knew the tune of the combination.

At this time, our main suspect in the case is Ms. Winslow's maintenance technician, 28-year-old Thomas Evans. Our investigators found high-tech computer and sound-recording equipment in Mr. Evans's apartment. Upon searching his hard drive, we discovered files containing digitized waveforms of a musical sequence.

We think Mr. Evans recorded the sounds made by the safe's keypad and used them to determine the combination of the lock. The computer files, along with the safe keypad, have been sent to the lab for analysis and comparison.

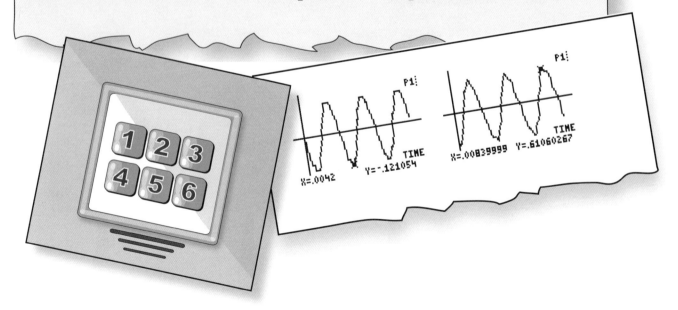

Forensics Objective

*   identify the musical notes that make up the combination to a safe

Science and Mathematics Objectives

*   detect the waveform of a musical note, using a Microphone
*   calculate the frequency of a musical note from the period of its waveform

Materials (for each group)

*   TI-83/TI-84 Plus™ Family
*   Calculator-Based Laboratory 2 ™ (CBL 2™) and link cable
*   Vernier EasyData™ application
*   Vernier Microphone
*   6 tuning forks of different frequencies
*   soft tuning-fork hammer

Procedure

1. Connect the CBL 2 to your calculator with the link cable.

2. Plug the Microphone probe into channel 1 (~CH1) of the CBL 2.

3. Load the EasyData application and set up to use the Microphone probe.
    a) Press (APPS).
    b) Use (▽) to highlight :EasyData. Press (ENTER) to start the application. The EasyData application will start automatically.

> At the bottom of the Main screen are five options ([File], [Setup], [Start], [Graph], and [Quit]). Each of these options can be selected by pressing the calculator key located below it ((Y=), (WINDOW), (ZOOM), (TRACE), or (GRAPH)).

4. Collect data to determine the frequency of each tuning fork. The easiest way to do this is to split up the group so that one person holds the tuning fork, a second person holds the Microphone, and a third controls the calculator.
    a) In the Evidence Record, write the number of the label found on the first tuning fork.
    b) Strike the tuning fork with the soft hammer and then hold the fork straight up and down.
    c) Hold the Microphone about 1 cm from the space between the prongs, as shown in the diagram below.

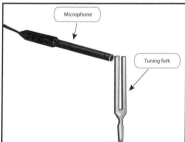

(Note: *Never* strike the tuning fork on a hard surface; it may change the waveform of the tuning fork.)

d) Select ⌈Start⌉ to start data collection. If you get a message about overwriting data, select ⌈OK⌉. The waveform will appear on your screen within a few seconds. It should look like one of the waveforms on the Waveforms of the Notes Taken from Evans's Computer Hard Drive handout. If it does not, repeat the analysis by selecting ⌈Main⌉ and repeating steps 4b–4c. Change the location of the vibrating tongs of the tuning fork until you get a clear waveform image. You will probably have to practice several times.

5. Once you have collected suitable data, you are ready to analyze the waveform to calculate the period and the frequency (or pitch) of the note.
   a) Press and hold ⊙ to move the cursor to a crest (highest point) of the waveform.
   b) At the bottom of the display, you will see **X=** and **Y=**. The **X=** is the time (in seconds). The **Y=** is the amplitude of the sound wave. Record the time, **X=**, displayed at the crest of the waveform as t_1 in the Evidence Record. Then move the cursor to the next crest, and record this time as t_2 in the Evidence Record. The value $t_2 - t_1$ is the period, T, of the note. Record the value you calculate for T in the Evidence Record.
   c) Calculate the frequency, f, of the note using the equation $f = \frac{1}{T}$. Record the frequency of the tuning fork in the Evidence Record. The unit for frequency is s^{-1} or hertz (Hz). One hertz equals one cycle per second.
   d) When you have finished analyzing the waveform, press ⟨ENTER⟩. Press ⟨2⟩ to repeat the analysis with another tuning fork.

6. Repeat steps 4 and 5 with the remaining tuning forks.

7. Calculate the period and frequency of each of the notes on the Waveforms of the Notes Taken from Evans's Computer Hard Drive handout, using the **X=** values shown as t_1 and t_2 for each pair of waveforms.

8. Compare the frequencies in the Evidence Record to the frequencies on Evans's computer hard drive. Determine the combination of notes that was stored on the hard drive, and record it in the Evidence Record.

Waveforms of the Notes Taken from Evans's Computer Hard Drive

First note

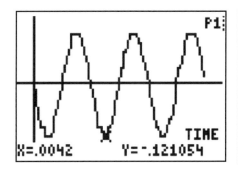 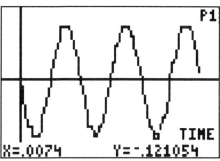

Period: _____

Frequency: _____

Note: _____

Second note

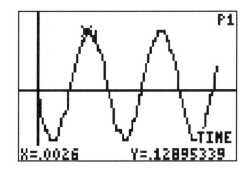 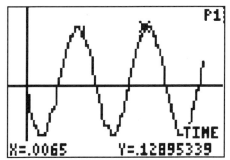

Period: _____

Frequency: _____

Note: _____

Third note

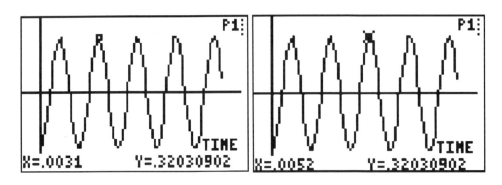

Period: _____

Frequency: _____

Note: _____

Fourth note

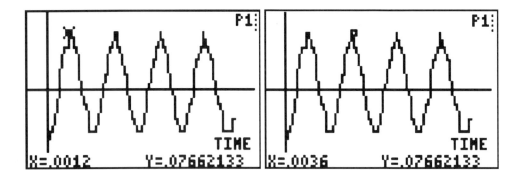

Period: _____

Frequency: _____

Note: _____

Fifth note

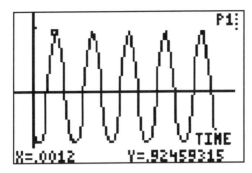 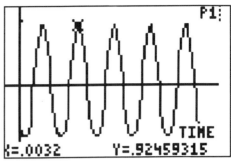

Period: _____

Frequency: _____

Note: _____

Sixth note

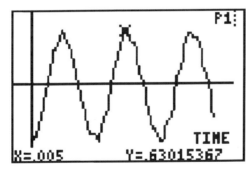 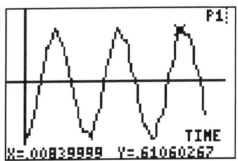

Period: _____

Frequency: _____

Note: _____

NAME: _____

DATE: _____

Evidence Record

Tuning Fork Number	Time at First Crest, t_1(s)	Time at Second Crest, t_2(s)	Period, T (s)	Frequency, f (cycles/s or Hz)

Order of tones in Evans's hard drive, using numbers on tuning forks: _____

Case Analysis

1. In step 5, you measured the time between two adjacent crests in the waveform of each tuning fork. However, some of the times that you calculated on the handout of Evans's hard drive were determined from two adjacent troughs (low points) in the waveforms. Explain why the period and frequency of a waveform calculated using the time between two crests are the same as when using two troughs.
2. Like all waves, sound waves have a frequency and a wavelength. The speed of sound in air is about 340 m/s. Frequency is measured in cycles per second. Speed is measured in meters per second. Wavelength is measured in meters.
   Using this information, write an equation that shows how you can calculate the wavelength of a wave if you know its frequency and speed.
3. Using the equation you wrote for question 2, calculate the wavelength of each of the notes produced by the tuning forks in your Evidence Record. Show all your work.
4. Using the same equation, explain how frequency and wavelength are related.
5. The police determined that the correct combination for the safe corresponded to the following order of wavelengths : _____.
   Did Evans record the safe combination, or was his recording of another combination of notes? How do you know?

Case File 3
Name That Tune: Matching musical tones through waveform analysis

Teacher Notes

Teaching time: one class period

In this activity, students analyze sound waves to calculate the frequency, or pitch, of musical notes.

Tips

* Note that EasyLink does not support the Microphone. To use the Microphone, you must have a CBL (Calculator-Based Laboratory).
* Before assigning the activity, you may want to review the basics of sound waves and the relationships between wavelength, period, frequency, and speed. Make sure students understand the relationship between pitch and frequency.
* Explain to the students that the calculated frequencies for the same tuning fork may vary by as much as 12 Hz. This is because the calculator rounds off the time between data points, introducing error into the measurements. For example, a period of 0.00195 s (frequency 513 Hz) would be recorded as 0.002 s by the calculator, giving a frequency of 500 Hz.
* Divide the class into groups of at least three students per group. It is easiest to perform the experiment if one person holds the tuning fork, one holds the Microphone, and one presses the keys on the calculator.
* Sometimes the fork works best when the base is sitting on a table and the hum is audible.
* The calculator also has a frequency function. Students may be tempted to use this function directly, rather than analyze the waveforms. However, without practice, it is difficult to get the right frequency using this function. The frequencies given are often multiples of the actual frequencies. If a student's data seem way off, this is probably the problem.
* Note that even when the fork appears to have become silent, it is still vibrating. You may or may not want to warn students that touching a vibrating tuning fork to teeth can break the teeth.

Lab Preparation

* Use a stick-on label to cover the identity and frequency of the note produced by each tuning fork, and assign each fork a number.
* You can use the following table to number the tuning forks. Provision has been made in the table for you to give different groups tuning forks that have different number schemes.

Note	Frequency (Hz)	Number for Group A	Number for Group B	Number for Group C	Number for Group D	Number for Group E	Number for Group F	Number for Group G
C	256	1	2	6	5	4	3	1
D	288	2	4	5	3	6	1	6
E	320	3	6	4	2	5	6	2
A	426.7	4	1	3	1	2	4	5
B	480	5	3	2	4	3	5	3
C	512	6	5	1	6	1	2	4

- The following table gives the safe combination for each group.

Group	Combination
A	3, 1, 5, 4, 6, 2
B	6, 2, 3, 1, 5, 4
C	4, 6, 2, 3, 1, 5
D	2, 5, 4, 1, 6, 3
E	5, 4, 3, 2, 1, 6
F	6, 3, 5, 4, 2, 1
G	2, 1, 3, 5, 4, 6

- You will need to tell the students the correct combination so that they can answer question 5 in the Case Analysis.

Background Information

All waves have three characteristic properties: wavelength, λ; frequency, f; and speed, v. These properties are related by the equation $v = f\lambda$. This equation can easily be obtained through unit analysis: wavelength has units of distance, frequency has units of inverse time (e.g., s^{-1} or Hz), and speed has units of distance per unit time. The wavelength of a wave is the distance between two successive peaks (crests) or valleys (troughs). The frequency is a measure of how many peaks or troughs pass a given point in a certain period of time (usually 1 second). Depending on the type of wave in question, wavelength and frequency can cause noticeable changes in the observable properties of the wave. For example, different wavelengths of visible light appear to have different colors, and different frequencies of sound waves have different pitches.

Resources

Tuning forks can be ordered from a science supply catalog or borrowed from the music department at your school.

Modifications

As an extension, or if tuning forks are not available, you may be able to use the notes produced by a touch-tone telephone. You may need to develop a new handout to accommodate the phone notes.

Sample Data

Waveforms of the Notes Taken from Evans's Computer Hard Drive

First note

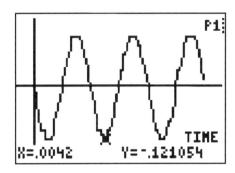 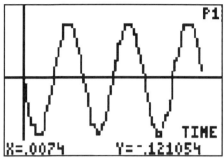

Period: <u>0.0032 s</u>

Frequency: <u>312 Hz</u>

Note: <u>E (320 Hz)</u>

Second note

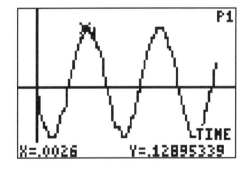 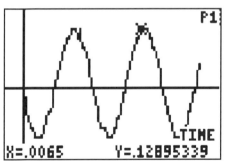

Period: <u>0.0039 s</u>

Frequency: <u>256 Hz</u>

Note: <u>C (256 Hz)</u>

Third note

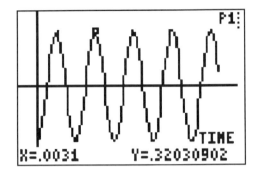 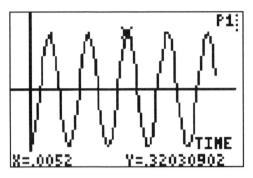

Period: <u>0.0021 s</u>

Frequency: <u>476 Hz</u>

Note: <u>B (480 Hz)</u>

Fourth note

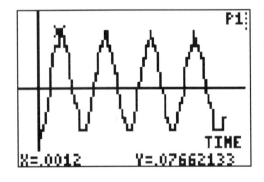 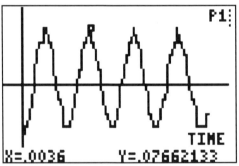

Period: <u>0.0024 s</u>

Frequency: <u>417 Hz</u>

Note: <u>A (426.7 Hz)</u>

Fifth note

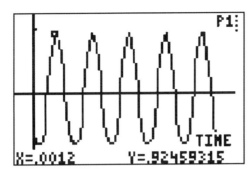 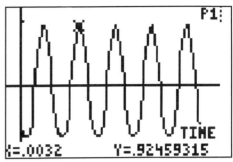

Period: <u>0.0020 s</u>

Frequency: <u>500 Hz</u>

Note: <u>C (512 Hz)</u>

Sixth note

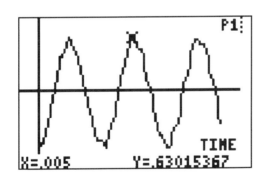 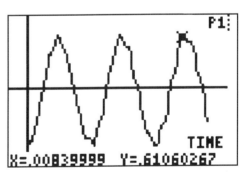

Period: <u>0.0034 s</u>

Frequency: <u>294 Hz</u>

Note: <u>D (288 Hz)</u>

The results in the following table use the tuning fork numbers for group A.

Tuning Fork Number	Time at First Crest, t_1(s)	Time at Second Crest, t_2(s)	Period, T (s)	Frequency, f (cycles/s or Hz)
1	0.003	0.0069	0.0039	256
2	0.0033	0.0066	0.0033	303
3	0.0025	0.0057	0.0032	313
4	0.0015	0.0038	0.0023	435
5	0.0016	0.0037	0.0021	476
6	0.0015	0.0035	0.0020	500

Order of tones in Evans's hard drive, using numbers on tuning forks:
 3, 1, 5, 4, 6, 2

Case Analysis Answers

1. In step 5, you measured the time between two adjacent crests in the waveform of each tuning fork. However, some of the times that you calculated on the handout of Evans's hard drive were determined from two adjacent troughs (low points) in the waveforms. Explain why the period and frequency of a waveform calculated using the time between two crests are the same as when using two troughs.
   Because waves are symmetrical, the distance between two adjacent troughs is the same as the distance between two adjacent crests.
2. Like all waves, sound waves have a frequency and a wavelength. The speed of sound in air is about 340 m/s. Frequency is measured in cycles per second. Speed is measured in meters per second. Wavelength is measured in meters.
   Using this information, write an equation that shows how you can calculate the wavelength of a wave if you know its frequency and speed.
   wavelength (m) = speed (m/s) ÷ frequency (cycles per second)
3. Using the equation you wrote for question 2, calculate the wavelength of each of the notes produced by the tuning forks in your Evidence Record. Show all your work.
   C (256 Hz) :   340 m/s ÷ 256/s = 1.3 m
   B (480 Hz) :   340 m/s ÷ 480/s = 0.71 m
   A (426.7 Hz):   340 m/s ÷ 426.7/s = 0.80 m
   E (320 Hz):   340 m/s ÷ 320/s = 1.1 m
   D (288 Hz):   340 m/s ÷ 288/s = 1.2 m
   C (512 Hz) :   340 m/s ÷ 512/s = 0.66 m
4. Using the same equation, explain how frequency and wavelength are related.
   As frequency increases, wavelength decreases (they are inversely related).
5. The police determined that the correct combination for the safe corresponded to the following order of wavelengths : _____.
   Did Evans record the safe combination, or was his recording of another combination of notes? How do you know?
   Answers will vary depending on whether or not you gave them the "correct" order of wavelengths for their particular numbered set of tuning forks.

Flipping Coins: Density as a characteristic property

Expose a counterfeiter by proving his "old" coins have a "new" density.

March 11

Times Standard

A Case of Coinery
Counterfeiting ring cracked

NEW THETFORDSHIRE, March 10: Coin collector Clark Esposito thought it was his lucky day when a stranger entered his shop with a plastic sleeve full of rare, mint 1877 indian head pennies. The seller, Zeus Duncan, said he had kept the coins in a locked safe since they were given to him by his father 20 years ago. However, Mr. Esposito's lucky day soon turned into a lucky break for police investigating a counterfeiting ring operating in the city.

"As soon as I picked up the sleeve, I knew something was wrong," said Mr. Esposito. "It was far too light to contain so many pennies." Fearing he was the target of a counterfeit operation, Mr. Esposito called the police, who arrived and took Mr. Duncan into custody. Police later proved that the coins were counterfeit. Instead of being genuine 1877 pennies, they were found to be modern pennies that had been re-stamped.

"This was the work of a master counterfeiter," says chief investigator Molly Harbert. "The 1877 indian head cent, when in good or mint condition, can sell for tens of thousands of dollars."

A real 1877 indian head cent (left) and one of the counterfeit pennies (right) are identical in size and relief.

Forensics Objective

- identify counterfeit coins based on the characteristic property of density

Science and Mathematics Objectives

- model data using a linear equation
- interpret the slope and intercept values from a linear model
- identify a characteristic property of a substance

Materials (for each group)

- TI-83/TI-84 Plus™Family
- Vernier EasyData™ application
- Vernier EasyLink™
- Dual-Range Force Sensor
- clamp or heavy tape
- light plastic coffee cup
- string
- 20 pennies dated 1963–1981
- 20 pennies dated 1982
- 20 pennies dated after 1982

Procedure

1. Set up your materials.
    a) Use a pencil to poke small holes on opposite sides of the coffee cup, near the top rim. Thread a piece of string through the holes, and then tie the ends of the string together to form a loop to hang the cup from.
    b) Separate each group of 20 pennies into four stacks of 5 pennies each. As you do this, confirm that you have 20 pre-1982 pennies, 20 pennies dated 1982, and 20 post-1982 pennies.
    c) Set the range switch on the Dual-Range Force Sensor to ±10 N.
    d) Secure the force sensor to the edge of a table. The sensor must be positioned with the hook closest to the ground and should remain level at all times. The diagram below gives an example of one way to set up the force sensor.

2. Plug the Dual-Range Force Sensor into EasyLink, and plug EasyLink into the USB port on the calculator. The calculator should automatically turn on and take you to the force sensor Main screen.

At the bottom of the Main screen are five options ($\boxed{\text{File}}$, $\boxed{\text{Setup}}$, $\boxed{\text{Start}}$, $\boxed{\text{Graph}}$, and $\boxed{\text{Quit}}$). Each of these options can be selected by pressing the calculator key located below it ($\boxed{\text{Y=}}$, $\boxed{\text{WINDOW}}$, $\boxed{\text{ZOOM}}$, $\boxed{\text{TRACE}}$, or $\boxed{\text{GRAPH}}$).

3. Notice that the mode on the bottom of your screen is **Time Graph**. You need to change this to **Events with Entry** so that you can tell the calculator when to record the force.
   a) Select $\boxed{\text{Setup}}$ from the Main screen.
   b) Select option **3: Events with Entry**. Your Main screen should now read **Events with Entry** on the bottom.

4. In this experiment, you want to measure the weight of the pennies only, not the pennies, cup, and string. To tell the calculator not to record the weight of the cup and string, you need to zero the force sensor.
   a) Hang the empty cup from the hook on the force sensor.
   b) Select $\boxed{\text{Setup}}$ and select option **7: Zero**.
   c) Wait until the reading is stable (make sure the cup is *not* moving). Select $\boxed{\text{Zero}}$ (not $\boxed{\text{0}}$) to zero the force sensor. This will set the current weight reading to 0, so the sensor will ignore the weight of the cup and the string.

5. You are now ready to record the weights of different numbers of pennies.
   a) The empty cup should be hanging from the hook on the force sensor. Select $\boxed{\text{Start}}$ to begin data collection.
   b) When the weight reading of the empty cup is stable (it should be very close to 0), select $\boxed{\text{Keep}}$.
   c) The calculator will then ask you to enter a value. Type **0** for the number of pennies now in the cup. Select $\boxed{\text{OK}}$ to store this weight-number data pair.
   d) Place five of the pre-1982 pennies in the cup, and wait until the reading is stable. Select $\boxed{\text{Keep}}$.
   e) Type **5** as the value for the number of pennies in the cup. Select $\boxed{\text{OK}}$ to store this weight-number data pair.
   f) Continue with this procedure, using increasing numbers of pre-1982 pennies. Each time you keep a data pair, enter the *total* number of pennies in the cup as the number value.
   g) Select $\boxed{\text{Stop}}$ when you have finished collecting data for the pre-1982 pennies.

6. The calculator screen will now show a graph with number of pennies on the *x*-axis and weight, in newtons, on the *y*-axis. The graph should appear linear (a straight line). If it does not, select $\boxed{\text{Main}}$ to return to the Main screen, and then repeat steps 4 and 5.

7. Determine the equation that describes the relationship between weight and number of pennies.
   a) Select $\boxed{\text{Anlyz}}$.
   b) Select option **2: Linear Fit**. This will tell the calculator to compute the equation of the straight line that best fits your data.
   c) The calculator will display values for **a**, **b**, and **R**. Record these values in the Evidence Record.
   d) The equation of a straight line is $y = ax + b$. Using the values shown on the screen, write the equation that best fits your data into your Evidence Record. (For example, if **a** = 3 and **b** = 5, the equation for the line is $y = 3x + 5$.)
   e) Select $\boxed{\text{OK}}$ to plot a line through the data points.
   f) Select $\boxed{\text{Main}}$ to return to the Main screen.

8. Repeat steps 4–7 for the pennies dated 1982.

9. Repeat steps 4–7 for the pennies dated after 1982.

NAME: _____

DATE: _____

Evidence Record

Penny Date	Equation of the Best Fit Line: $y = ax + b$
1963–1981	a: _____ b: _____ R: _____ Equation ($y = ax + b$): _____
1982	a: _____ b: _____ R: _____ Equation ($y = ax + b$): _____
After 1982	a: _____ b: _____ R: _____ Equation ($y = ax + b$): _____

Case Analysis

1. The equation for a straight line is $y = ax + b$, where x and y are coordinates on the line, a is the slope of the line, and b is the y-intercept (the value of y when $x = 0$).
    In this case, y is the weight of the pennies, in newtons, x is the number of pennies, and a is the "density" of the pennies. What are the units of "density" in this equation?
2. Explain why the y-intercept, b, should be 0.
3. Was the value of b that you recorded for each group of pennies equal to 0? If not, explain why not.
4. How do the "densities" of the three sets of pennies compare? Based on your measurements, what do you think probably happened to the composition of the penny in 1982?
5. Use the appropriate equation to determine the weight of 5000 pennies from 1980. Show the equation you used and how you rearranged and/or substituted into the equation. Underline your answer.
6. Use the appropriate equation to determine the weight of 5000 pennies from 2005. Show the equation you used and how you rearranged and/or substituted into the equation. Underline your answer.
7. In this activity, "density" is in quotation marks because the slope of the line, a, is not actually density; a is just a *measure* of density. Explain why the value of a is not really density.

8. Why can you still use slope, a, as a measure of density?
9. What could have made the penny "densities" you calculated inaccurate?
10. From 1864 to 1962, pennies were made of 95% copper and 5% zinc-tin alloy. From 1962 to 1981, pennies were made of 95% copper and 5% zinc. Since 1983, pennies have been made of 97.5% *zinc* and 2.5% *copper*. Zinc is significantly less dense than copper. Tin is slightly more dense than zinc but still much less dense than copper.

    If the suspect's coins are genuine 1877 pennies, how should their density compare with the densities of the pennies you measured in this activity?
11. Police measured the weight of five of the suspect's coins and found them to be 0.06 N (about 0.22 oz) each. Based on the data you collected, explain how the police knew that the suspect's coins were fakes. (Hint: What is the weight of five pennies from after 1982?)
12. R is a measure of how well the line fits the data points. A large value of R indicates that the line is a good fit to the data points. Which group of pennies showed the best fit to a straight line? How do you know?

Case File 4
Flipping Coins: Density as a characteristic property

Teacher Notes

Teaching time: one class period

This lab introduces the concept of density and uses it to distinguish between pennies minted in different years.

Tips

- Before assigning this activity, you may want to review the concept of density, the formula for density (mass divided by volume), and the equation of a line ($y = ax+b$).
- If pennies are scarce, have groups share batches.
- It is important that the force sensor be firmly attached to a stationary object; it will probably not give good results if you have a student hold it. You may need to experiment a bit to devise a mechanism to hold the force sensor in place on the tables available in your classroom; the image given in the procedure is just a suggestion.

Background Information

As shown in the table below, the U.S. Department of the Treasury has changed the composition, and thus the density, of the penny several times.

Date	Penny Composition
1793–1837	Pure copper
1837–1857	95% copper, 5% tin and zinc
1857–1864	88% copper, 12% nickel
1864–1942	95% copper, 5% tin and zinc
1943	Zinc-coated steel; pure copper in a few
1944–1962	95% copper, 5% tin and zinc
1962–1982	95% copper, 5% zinc
1982–present	97.5% zinc, 2.5% copper (copper-coated zinc)

Source: http://www.usmint.gov/about_the_mint/fun_facts/index.cfm?flash=yes&action=fun_facts2

Metal	Density (g/cm³)
Copper	8.92
Nickel	8.91
Tin	7.31
Zinc	7.14

The general equation for the density of a coin is the following:

density = [(percentage of metal A) × (density of metal A)]
+ [(percentage of metal B) × (density of metal B)]

Density of pennies from 1963 to 1981 =
(0.95) (8.92 g/cm³) + (0.05) (7.14 g/cm³) = 8.83 g/cm³

Density of pennies since 1983 =
(0.975) (7.14 g/cm³) + (0.025) (8.92 g/cm³) = 7.18 g/cm³

The composition was changed in 1982 because the cost of making the penny was more than the penny was worth!

Modifications

- If you have trouble finding enough 1982 pennies, students can skip step 8.
- If students are having trouble understanding how to interpret the equations that the calculator generates, you may want to have them sketch and label the graphs in step 6.
- Advanced students can use the chemical composition and density data in the Background Information to calculate and compare the densities of pennies minted in different years and then compare those densities to their experimental data. Depending on how advanced the students are, you may have them research the penny compositions and metal density information themselves. It is important that they understand that the slope of the weight–number-of-pennies line is *not* actually density (see Case Analysis questions 7 and 8).
- Advanced students can try to convert the units of a (newtons per penny) to the standard density units (g/cm³). Students can also try to determine the volume of a penny (they will need to convert weight to mass and use the calculated density of a penny).

Sample Data

Penny Date	Equation of the Best Fit Line: $y = ax + b$
1963–1981	a = 0.02969694 b = -0.0095746 R = 0.99792326 Equation ($y = ax + b$): $y = 0.02969694x + (-0.0095746)$
1982	a = 0.02384556 b = -0.0105673 R = 0.99629841 Equation ($y = ax + b$): $y = 0.02384556x + (-0.0105673)$
After 1982	a = 0.01862232 b = -0.0332276 R = 0.99313258 Equation ($y = ax + b$): $y = 0.01862232x + (-0.0332276)$

Case Analysis Answers

1. The equation for a straight line is $y = ax + b$, where x and y are coordinates on the line, a is the slope of the line, and b is the y-intercept (the value of y when $x = 0$).
   In this case, y is the weight of the pennies, in newtons, x is the number of pennies, and a is the "density" of the pennies. What are the units of "density" in this equation?
   These units are newtons per penny.

2. Explain why the y-intercept, b, should be 0.
   When $x = 0$, there are no pennies being measured. The weight of no pennies should be 0.

3. Was the value of b that you recorded for each group of pennies equal to 0? If not, explain why not.
   Answers will vary. Possible reasons for non-zero b values include air currents in the room or movement of the force sensor. It is difficult to collect the first point exactly when the force sensor measures 0.

4. How do the "densities" of the three sets of pennies compare? Based on your measurements, what do you think probably happened to the composition of the penny in 1982?
   The pennies minted before 1982 are denser than the pennies minted after 1982. The density of pennies minted in 1982 falls between the other two groups. The composition of the penny was probably changed in 1982 in a way that made it less dense.

5. Use the appropriate equation to determine the weight of 5000 pennies from 1980. Show the equation you used and how you rearranged and/or substituted into the equation. Underline your answer.

   $$y = 0.02969694 \, x - 0.0095746$$
   $$y = 0.02969694 \, (5000) - 0.0095746 = \underline{148 \, N}$$

6. Use the appropriate equation to determine the weight of 5000 pennies from 2005. Show the equation you used and how you rearranged and/or substituted into the equation. Underline your answer.

$$y = 0.01862232 \, x - 0.0332276$$
$$y = 0.01862232 \, (5000) - 0.0332276 = \underline{93 \, N}$$

7. In this case, "density" is in quotation marks because the slope of the line, a, is not actually density; a is just a *measure* of density. Explain why the value of a is not really density.
   Density is mass divided by volume. The a here equals weight (force, in newtons) divided by number of pennies. Although a penny is essentially a unit of volume, weight is not the same thing as mass.

8. Why can you use a here as a measure of density?
   You can use weight divided by number because you can assume that the ratio of weight to mass does not, change and that every penny has the same volume, regardless of the year it was minted. (The ratio of weight to mass does not change because weight is a measure of the force of gravity on a mass. Because every penny is in the same place, the force of gravity is the same on each, so only the mass affects the measured weight.)

9. What can make the penny "densities" you calculate inaccurate?
   The pennies may be worn down and so have less volume. If they are corroded, they may have slightly different compositions. If the force sensor is not kept stable, the readings can be inaccurate.

10. From 1864 to 1962, pennies were made of 95% copper and 5% zinc-tin alloy. From 1962 to 1981, pennies were made of 95% copper and 5% zinc. Since 1983, pennies have been made of 97.5% *zinc* and 2.5% *copper*. Zinc is significantly less dense than copper. Tin is slightly more dense than zinc but still much less dense than copper.
    If the suspect's coins are genuine 1877 pennies, how should their density compare with the densities of the pennies you measured in this activity?
    They should be more dense than any of the pennies in the activity.

11. Police weighed the suspect's coins and found that five of them weighed 0.06 N (about 0.22 oz). Based on the data you collected, explain how the police knew that the suspect's coins were fakes. (Hint: What is the weight of five pennies from after 1982?)
    Five pennies from 1877 should weigh significantly more than 0.06 N, which is the approximate weight of five pennies from 2005. Therefore, the suspect's pennies were fakes.

12. R is a measure of how well the line fits the data points. A large value of R indicates that the line is a good fit to the data points. Which group of pennies showed the best fit to a straight line? How do you know?
    Answers will vary. In the case of the sample data, the 1963–1981 pennies showed the best fit (the largest value of R).

The Ink Is Still Wet: Using colorimetry to identify an unknown ink

Identify the ink on the ransom note to narrow down the suspects.

Springfie

4

TrueMind AI Kidnapping Case Solved!
Mystery ink proves key to case

SPRINGFIELD, September 10: Science has proven indispensable in solving yet another kidnapping case. This time, a special kind of fingerprint—a chemical fingerprint—proved to be the crucial clue in recovering the victim, 22-year-old Shawn Morgan, unharmed.

It was only in the last month that Morgan sold his design for the TrueMind artificial intelligence system to the United States government for $100 million. As fate would have it, a day later, Morgan vanished. When investigators forcibly entered Mr. Morgan's apartment, they found it empty except for a ransom note written on a piece of computer paper. The note was written in black ink, and the handwriting varied in style, so police handwriting experts were at a loss to come up with a profile.

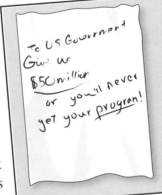

To US Government
Give us
$50 million
or you'll never
get your program!

Using advanced chemical analysis, investigators determined that the ink used to write the infamous "To US Government" ransom note came from a specialized marker used in photo retouching. These pens are unusual and unusually expensive, and investigators found one at the apartment of one of the prime suspects, Tamyra Elliot, 32. Ms. Elliot is currently being held without bail.

continued on p. C4

Forensics Objective

- identify an unknown ink by its light absorbance characteristics

Science and Mathematics Objective

- measure a solution's absorbance of different colors (wavelengths) of light

Materials (for each group)

- TI-83/TI-84 Plus™ Family
- Vernier EasyLink™
- Vernier EasyData™ application
- Colorimeter
- 6 cuvettes
- colored wax pencil
- 5 dropper bottles, with 10 mL samples of 5 different diluted black inks
- 1 dropper bottle with 10 mL of diluted unknown black ink
- deionized or distilled water
- lint-free tissues
- goggles (1 pair per student)

Procedure

Wear goggles at all times! CAUTION: Be careful not to ingest any solution or spill any on your skin. Inform your teacher immediately in the event of an accident.

1. Prepare the blank, each of the five standards, and the unknown for analysis.
   a) Rinse an empty cuvette twice with about 1 mL of distilled or deionized water.
   b) Use the colored wax pencil to write a zero on the lid of the cuvette.
   c) Fill the cuvette three-fourths full with deionized water. Seal the cuvette with the lid. Dry the outside of the cuvette with a tissue.
   d) Repeat steps 1a–1c, using the five standard solutions and the unknown, rather than deionized water, and labeling the lids of the cuvettes appropriately (1 through 5 for the standard solutions and 6 for the unknown).
   Remember the following:
   - All cuvettes should be clean and dry on the outside.
   - Handle a cuvette only by the top edge or ribbed sides, not the transparent sides.
   - All solutions should be free of bubbles.
   - Label the *lid* of the cuvette so the label does not interfere with the beam of light.

2. Connect EasyLink to the USB port of your calculator, and connect the Colorimeter to EasyLink. The EasyData App should open automatically.

3. Set up EasyData to collect absorbance readings.
   a) Select ⌈File⌉ from the Main screen, and then select option **1: New** to reset the application.
   b) Select ⌈Setup⌉ from the Main screen, and then select option **3: Events with Entry**.

4. Calibrate the Colorimeter.
   a) Place the blank (cuvette 0, containing deionized water) in the cuvette slot of the Colorimeter. Make sure that one of the transparent faces of the cuvette is pointing toward the white reference mark. Close the lid of the Colorimeter.
   b) Set the wavelength on the Colorimeter to 635 nm (red).

    c)   Calibrate the Colorimeter by pressing the CAL button.

    d)   Remove the blank cuvette from the Colorimeter.

5. You are now ready to collect absorbance-concentration data at 635 nm for the solutions.

    a)   Place cuvette 1 in the Colorimeter, with the cuvette clean, dry, and with a transparent face pointing toward the reference mark.

    b)   Select ⌜Start⌝ to begin data collection.

    c)   When the value displayed on the calculator screen has stabilized, select ⌜Keep⌝ to record the absorbance of the first standard, or known sample.

    d)   The screen will ask you for a value. Enter the sample number (from the lid) and select ⌜OK⌝ to store this absorbance–sample-number data pair.

    e)   Remove the cuvette from the Colorimeter.

    f)   Repeat steps 5a–5e for the remaining samples in cuvettes 2 through 6.

6. Select ⌜Stop⌝ when you have collected data for all the samples. EasyData should display a graph of the data.

7. Examine the data points along the curve on the displayed graph. As you move the cursor right or left, the sample number, **X**, and absorbance value, **Y**, of each data point are displayed above the graph. Write the absorbance values in your Evidence Record (round to the nearest 0.001).

8. Select ⌜Main⌝ to return to the Main screen.

9. Measure the absorbance of each solution at the three other wavelengths (or colors) that the Colorimeter can measure.

    a)   Repeat steps 4–8 for the 565 nm (green) wavelength setting on the Colorimeter.

    b)   Repeat steps 4–8 for the 470 nm (blue) wavelength setting on the Colorimeter.

    c)   Repeat steps 4–8 for the 430 nm (violet) wavelength setting on the Colorimeter.

10. Discard the solutions as directed by your teacher.

NAME: _____

DATE: _____

Evidence Record

Sample	Type of Ink; Appearance in Alcohol	Absorbance at 635 nm	Absorbance at 565 nm	Absorbance at 470 nm	Absorbance at 430 nm
1					
2					
3					
4					
5					
6	Unknown				

Unknown is most likely _____

Case Analysis

1. How did you identify the unknown?
2. Why did the inks show different absorbance patterns if they all appeared to be the same color?
3. Do you think you would have seen the same large variations in absorbance if all the samples had been red ink or all had been blue ink instead of black? Why or why not?

Case File 5
The Ink Is Still Wet: Using colorimetry to identify an unknown ink

Teacher Notes

Teaching time: one class period

This lab utilizes colorimetry to identify inks as unique mixtures of pigments.

Tips

- Use of the Colorimeter with the calculator is extremely battery intensive. Keep extra batteries on hand. You should make sure that all solution preparation and cuvette filling is done *before* turning on the Colorimeter in order to minimize the battery drain on the calculator.
- Before assigning the lab, you may want to review the spectrum of visible light and the concept of absorbance of light. Remind students that different colors are actually different wavelengths in the spectrum and that an object appears to be a specific color because it absorbs all wavelengths of light *except* that specific color. It may also be helpful to review the difference between colors of light (white light is a combination of all wavelengths, and darkness is the absence of all wavelengths) and colors of pigment (white pigment *reflects* all wavelengths, and black pigment *absorbs* all wavelengths).

Lab Preparation

- Use rubber gloves to prepare all the ink solutions.
- Use five different brands of pens (e.g., Pilot, Bic, Zebra) and/or different types of pens (e.g., erasable ink, archival ink) for the known solutions. Use one of those five for the unknown.
- To prepare each ink solution, disassemble the pen (or purchase a refill ink cartridge), cut the ink cylinder, and put the cylinder parts into alcohol to allow the ink to dissolve in it. Each ink will dissolve at a different rate, so the soak times will vary.
- Prepare each dropper bottle sample by diluting an ink-and-alcohol sample with deionized water. The six different diluted samples should look similar. Of the black inks used to obtain the sample data, the Bic, Pentel, and Zebra had a purplish hue and were indistinguishable from one another when diluted; the Pilot ink was black in dilution; ink from the erasable Paper Mate was blue in dilution.

Background Information

The Colorimeter works by passing a beam of a single wavelength of light through the sample and then measuring how much of that light is transmitted. The Colorimeter can then calculate how much of that wavelength was absorbed by the sample. This technique can help identify materials because different materials absorb different amounts of light at different wavelengths.

Most inks are mixtures of different-colored pigments. When we separate those mixtures, we can define their parts, and the percentages of the parts allow us to identify the original ink. Many companies have their own formulas for the inks that they use. Each pigment has distinctive spectral properties. We can see those properties when we examine the solutions in light of different wavelengths.

Resources

http://chemistry.about.com/library/weekly/aa121602a.htm
This Web site contains information about the properties of different inks.

Modifications

More-advanced students may want to explore the absorbance of different-colored inks (red, blue, green) to see if the variations in absorbance pattern are as great as they are for black inks.

Sample Data (using pens that write in black)

Sample	Type of Ink; Appearance in Alcohol	Absorbance at 635 nm	Absorbance at 565 nm	Absorbance at 470 nm	Absorbance at 430 nm
1	Pilot gel ink; black	0.408	0.498	0.539	0.492
2	Paper Mate erasable; blue	0.951	0.986	0.958	0.926
3	Bic; purple	0.278	0.681	0.433	0.402
4	Pentel; purple	0.111	0.355	0.217	0.182
5	Zebra; purple	0.181	0.379	0.262	0.241
6	**Unknown;** purple	0.288	0.673	0.437	0.395

Unknown is most likely _____3 Bic_____

Case Analysis Answers

1. How did you identify the unknown?
    I found the set of absorbances that most closely matched those of the unknown.
2. Why did the inks show different absorbance patterns if they all appeared to be the same color?
    Even though the inks are the same color, the amount of colorant(s) and the kind of colorant(s) present may vary, causing the absorbance readings to vary.
3. Do you think you would have seen the same large variations in absorbance if all the samples had been red ink or all had been blue ink instead of black? Why or why not?
    The variations in absorbance patterns would probably have been smaller if we had used red or blue ink because those inks tend to be mixtures of fewer pigments.

Case File 6

Measuring Momentum: Using distance moved after impact to estimate velocity

Explore how the speed of an impacting vehicle causes a stationary object to move.

Police Report

Last Tuesday night, police officers were dispatched to the remote icy intersection of Elm Road and Winding Way for a routine collision investigation. The driver of a car seems to have lost control of his vehicle on the ice and crashed into a black van sitting idle on the side of the road.

Investigators took some measurements at the crime scene in order to determine how fast the car was going before it hit the van. Since the car skidded on an icy road, there were no tire tracks to measure to determine its speed. However, the van was parked on a sandy shoulder, and investigators were able to measure the distance it was pushed when the car hit it.

The marks in the sand show that the van was pushed 1.6 meters when it was struck by the car. According to the car manufacturer, the car has a mass of 1000 kg.

Forensics Objective

- establish a relationship between the momentum of a vehicle and the distance a stationary object moves when the vehicle hits it

Science and Mathematics Objectives

- accurately gather data from a collision of a vehicle with a stationary object
- establish a relationship between the distance an object moves after a collision with a vehicle and the momentum of the vehicle

Materials (for each group)

- TI-83/TI-84 Plus™ Family
- Vernier EasyData™ application
- Vernier EasyLink™
- Dual-Range Force Sensor
- Calculator-Based Ranger 2™ (CBR 2™)
- clamp or heavy tape
- 1.5 m (or longer) ramp of strong cardboard or wood
- meterstick
- 25 cm (or higher) support for ramp
- masking tape
- 450–500 g vehicle about 7 cm tall
- book, 5–7 cm thick
- book, 2 cm thick
- string or wide rubber band

Procedure

1. Set the switch on the Dual-Range Force Sensor to ±10 N. Plug the force sensor into EasyLink, and plug EasyLink into the calculator. The calculator should automatically turn on and take you to the Main screen for the force sensor.

2. Hold the force sensor vertically with the hook pointing down. Hang a rubber band or string from the hook.

3. Select ⌈Setup⌉ and choose option **7: Zero**. When the weight has stabilized, select ⌈Zero⌉ (not ⌈ 0 ⌉). This will zero the sensor for weighing the objects with the rubber band or string attached.

At the bottom of the Main screen are five options (⌈File⌉, ⌈Setup⌉, ⌈Start⌉, ⌈Graph⌉, and ⌈Quit⌉). Each of these options can be selected by pressing the calculator key located below it (⌈ Y= ⌉, ⌈WINDOW⌉, ⌈ZOOM⌉, ⌈TRACE⌉, or ⌈GRAPH⌉).

4. Calculate the mass of the vehicle that you will be using to collide with the books.
   a) Hang the vehicle from the force sensor with the string or rubber band. The weight of the vehicle, in newtons, will be displayed on the top of the screen. Record this number in your Evidence Record.
   b) Convert the weight to mass, using the equation below, and record it in your Evidence Record.

$$\text{Mass in kilograms} = \frac{\text{Weight in newtons}}{\text{Acceleration due to gravity } (9.8 \, \text{m/sec}^2)}$$

5. Weigh and calculate the mass of each of the books, and record the numbers in your Evidence Record.

6. Unplug the force sensor from the calculator's USB port.

7. Set up the ramp as shown in the figure below. Place the heavier (thicker) of the two books at the base of the ramp.

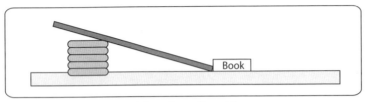

View from the side

8. With the book at the bottom of the ramp, place the vehicle at the bottom of the ramp against the book. Apply a strip of tape to the ramp at the location of the front wheels of the vehicle. The tape should be about 10 cm long and parallel to the bottom edge of the ramp.

9. Place a meterstick in the center of the ramp with the 0 at the bottom edge of the tape you applied in step 8. Tape it securely to the ramp at the following distances: 25, 35, 50, 70, and 80 cm from the bottom edge of the tape, as shown in the figure below. The meterstick will provide an additional support for a cardboard ramp, a guide for the vehicle, and a way to measure the distance the vehicle will travel down the ramp.

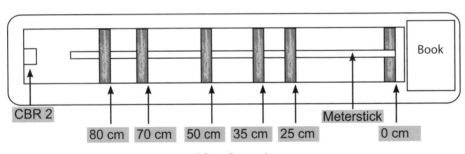

View from above

10. Firmly attach the CBR 2 cable to the USB port of your calculator. This will automatically start the EasyData App. Distance data will be displayed at the top of the screen.

11. Change the timed-experiment parameters to record one sample every 0.05 seconds for 2 seconds.
    a) Select [Setup] from the Main screen.
    b) Select option **2: Time Graph**, and then select [Edit].
    c) Press (CLEAR) and then type **0.05** as the sample interval. Select [Next].
    d) Press (CLEAR) and then type **40** for the number of samples. Select [Next].
    e) When you have confirmed that the time graph settings are correct (0.05-second sample interval, 40 samples, 2-second experiment length), select [OK].

12. Place the CBR 2 at the top of the ramp. There should be at least 25 cm between the CBR 2 and the rear of the vehicle when the vehicle is placed with its front wheels at the 80 cm mark.

13. Place the vehicle on the ramp so that it straddles the meterstick and has its front wheels at the 80 cm mark.

14. Select ⌈**Start**⌉ to begin data collection. (Note: You may also have to select ⌈**OK**⌉ to overwrite old data.) Release the vehicle about half a second after you hear the rapid clicking sound made by the CBR 2.

15. When the vehicle has collided with the book and the CBR 2 has stopped clicking, the calculator will plot a distance vs. time graph on the screen. It should look similar to the one shown below. (Note: Do not be confused by any unusual distance readings that may show up on the graph for times after the vehicle has collided with the book. Focus on the data collected only up to the point that the vehicle struck the book.)

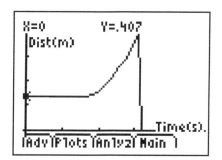

Determine the vehicle's velocity when it struck the book.

a) Select ⌈**Plots**⌉ from the Main screen and choose option **2:Vel(m/s) vs Time**. Your velocity vs. time graph should be similar to the graph below. The velocity when the vehicle was at the end of the ramp will be the maximum point on the graph. (Note: Again, do not be confused by any unusual velocity readings on this graph for times after the vehicle collided with the book.)

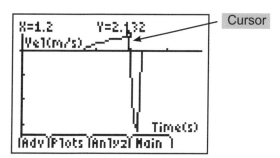

b) Move your cursor to the point corresponding to the time when the vehicle struck the book. Record the velocity of the vehicle at this point. The velocity is the *y*-value shown at the top of the screen. Record this velocity in your Evidence Record. If your graph does not have a clear maximum point, repeat steps 13–15. You may need to make several runs to get good results.

16. Measure the distance the book was pushed by its collision with the vehicle. Enter that distance in *meters* into your Evidence Record. If the book was not pushed parallel to the ramp, measure the distance from its starting point to the edge of the book along its centerline, as shown in the figure below. Once you have measured the distance, return the book to its original position at the base of the ramp.

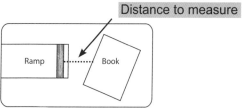

Distance to measure, Book, Ramp

17. Repeat steps 13–16 twice more. Calculate the average of the results and record it in the Evidence Record.

18. Repeat steps 13–17 for the other distances you have marked off on your ramp (70, 50, 35, and 25 cm).

19. Repeat steps 13–18 for the lighter (thinner) book.

20. Calculate the average momentum of the vehicle at impact for each average distance the book moved. Do this by multiplying the average speed (velocity) of the vehicle by the mass of the vehicle. Record the average momentums in the Evidence Record.

21. Enter the momentum and distance data for the *heavy* book into lists in the calculator.
    a) Exit EasyData by selecting ⌈Quit⌉ then ⌈OK⌉.
    b) Press ⟨STAT⟩ ⟨ENTER⟩ to open the list editor. If any of the lists already contain data, use the arrow keys to highlight the title of the list and press ⟨CLEAR⟩ ⟨ENTER⟩ to erase all the old data in the list.
    c) In the first list, L1, enter the average momentum of the vehicle that you calculated for each incline distance (distance vehicle traveled).
    d) Use the arrow to move over to the second list, L2, and enter the average distance that the heavy book moved for each incline distance.

22. Plot a graph of the distance the heavy book moved versus the momentum of the vehicle at impact.
    a) Press ⟨2nd⟩ ⟨Y=⟩ to enter the **STAT PLOT** menu.
    b) Press ⟨ENTER⟩ to select **Plot 1**. Use the arrow keys to highlight **On**, and then press ⟨ENTER⟩ to select.
    c) Use the arrow keys to highlight the first type of graph, a dot (scatter) plot, and then press ⟨ENTER⟩ to select.
    d) Use the arrow keys to highlight the entry next to **Xlist:**. Press ⟨2nd⟩ ⟨1⟩ to select list **L1**. This will tell the calculator to plot momentum (list L1) on the x-axis.
    e) Use the arrow keys to highlight the entry next to **Xlist:**. Press ⟨2nd⟩ ⟨2⟩ to select list **L2**. This will tell the calculator to plot distance (list L2) on the y-axis.
    f) Use the arrow keys to highlight the entry next to **Mark:**. Highlight the first mark and press ⟨ENTER⟩ to select.
    g) Press ⟨ZOOM⟩ and select option **9↓:ZoomStat** to automatically scale your graph.
    h) Your screen should now show a graph of the vehicle's momentum on the x-axis and the distance it pushed the book on the y-axis.

23. You will be using the calculator's LinReg program to determine the equation for the straight line that fits your data best. A linear regression is a mathematical formula that can be used to do this. (Note: It is possible to calculate the equation by hand, but it takes a long time and is tedious. Your calculator has a program called LinReg that will calculate it quickly.) Turn on the calculator's **Diagnostic** function. This will tell the calculator to determine how well the line fits the data, in addition to calculating the equation for the line.
    a) Go to the calculator's function catalog by pressing ⟨2nd⟩ ⟨0⟩.
    b) Use the arrow keys to scroll down to the **DiagnosticOn** option, and then press ⟨ENTER⟩ ⟨ENTER⟩ to select it and turn it on.

24. Use the LinReg function to perform the linear regression and store the resulting equation in variable **Y1**:
    a) Press ⟨STAT⟩, highlight **CALC**, and choose option **4: LinReg(ax + b)**. The Home screen will read **LinReg(ax + b)**. (Do *not* press ⟨ENTER⟩ yet.)
    b) You need to tell the calculator where your data are and where to store the final equation. Press ⟨2nd⟩ ⟨1⟩ ⟨,⟩ ⟨2nd⟩ ⟨2⟩ ⟨,⟩ to tell the calculator that lists L1 and L2 contain the data that you want to fit a line to. (Do *not* press ⟨ENTER⟩ yet.)

c) To indicate that you want to store the equation in variable Y1, press ⬭VARS ⬭▸ to select **Y-VARS**. Press ⬭ENTER ⬭ENTER to tell the calculator to store the equation in the **Y1** variable. The Main screen should now read **LinReg(ax+b) L1,L2,Y1**.

25. Now press ⬭ENTER to execute the LinReg function. This function calculates the equation for the straight line that fits through your data best. The screen will display the values for a and b that make the linear equation fit the data. The r^2 value tells you how well the line fits the data. An r^2 value that is close to 1 means that the line fits the data very well. Fill in the LinReg (Heavy Book) table in the Evidence Record.

26. Press ⬭GRAPH. You should see your graph and a best fit line being drawn through the points. Sketch the graph of distance vs. momentum data in the Evidence Record.

27. Press ⬭2nd ⬭MODE to quit the graph screen and go back to the Home screen. Repeat steps 21–26 for the *light* book.

Name: _____

Date: _____

Evidence Record

Weight of vehicle _____ N
Mass of vehicle   _____ kg

For the Heavy Book

Weight of book _____ N
Mass of book   _____ kg

Distance Vehicle Traveled Before Colliding with Book (m)	Velocity of Vehicle (m/sec)	Distance Book Moved (m)
0.8		
0.8		
0.8		
0.7		
0.7		
0.7		
0.5		
0.5		
0.5		
0.35		
0.35		
0.35		
0.25		
0.25		
0.25		

Distance Vehicle Traveled Before Colliding with Book (m)	Average Velocity of Vehicle (m/sec)	Average Distance Book Moved (m)	Average Momentum of Vehicle at Impact (kg·m/sec)
0.8			
0.7			
0.5			
0.35			
0.25			

LinReg (Heavy Book)

Sketch of graph of distance vs. momentum data

y	$ax + b$
a	
b	
r^2	

For the Light Book

Weight of book _____ N
Mass of book _____ kg

Distance Vehicle Traveled Before Colliding with Book (m)	Velocity of Vehicle (m/sec)	Distance Book Moved (m)
0.8		
0.8		
0.8		
0.7		
0.7		
0.7		
0.5		
0.5		
0.5		
0.35		
0.35		
0.35		
0.25		
0.25		
0.25		

Distance Vehicle Traveled Before Colliding with Book (m)	Average Velocity of Vehicle (m/sec)	Average Distance Book Moved (m)	Average Momentum of Vehicle at Impact (kg·m/sec)
0.8			
0.7			
0.5			
0.35			
0.25			

LinReg (Light Book)

y	ax + b
a	
b	
r^2	

Sketch of graph of distance vs. momentum data

Case Analysis

1. Is the linear regression a good fit to the data for the heavy book? For the light book? Explain.
2. For the *heavy* book, write the equation for the distance vs. momentum graph. Use $y = ax + b$ and values from step 25. The y is distance the book moved, and x is momentum at impact.
3. Using your equation, calculate how far the book would move if its momentum at impact were 0.7 kg·m/sec. Show your work. Don't forget that your answer has units.
4. If the book moved 0.2 m after impact, what would the momentum of the vehicle have been when it hit the book? Show your work.
5. Repeat questions 3 and 4 for the *light* book.
6. The equation for the accident scene is $y = 0.00245x - 37.8$, where y is distance the van moved (in meters) and x is momentum of the car at impact (in kg·m/s). What was the car's momentum just before it hit the van? (Hint: Rearrange the equation to solve for x.) Show your work.
7. What was the impact velocity of the car in meters per second? Show your work. (Hint: Rearrange the momentum equation, $p = m \cdot v$ where p is momentum, m is mass, and v is velocity. Then substitute for momentum, from question 6, and mass of the car, 1000 kg.)
8. If the speed limit on the road was 50 mph, was the car speeding just before it hit the van? Show your work. (Hint: Multiply velocity in meters per second, from the last question, by 2.24.)

Case File 6
Measuring Momentum: Using momentum to determine intent

Teacher Notes

Teaching time: one or two class periods

This lab introduces the concept of momentum as it applies to vehicle collisions.

Tips

- Test the setup to be sure that the vehicle will move the books a measurable distance from all of the designated points on the ramp. If this does not happen, add some weight to the vehicle or use a lighter book.
- If a Dual-Range Force Sensor is not available, use a pan balance or spring scale to find the mass of the books and vehicle directly.
- When taping the meterstick to the ramp, make sure that the tape does not interfere with the movement of the vehicle's wheels.

Lab Preparation

Materials
- A 1.5 m piece of corrugated board can very likely be found at a furniture or grocery store. If you are unable to locate a piece of corrugated board, a thin piece of paneling cut to 1.5 m × 40 cm will also work as a ramp.
- If you are using a toy truck, two metersticks taped to the ramp may be a better guide for the truck.
- If you have access to a Vernier® Dynamics System, the cart from that system, with a 3 × 5 inch card taped to the rear of the cart (to reflect the sound waves), works well.

Setup Information
- It is best to run this activity on a smooth surface, such as an uncarpeted floor or smooth table. The lower the coefficient of friction between the book and the surface, the better the data.
- Collecting good data for the velocity of the vehicle and the distance the book moves (it may move on the diagonal) can take a lot of time. If you have two ramps and similar vehicles, it may be a good idea to have two teams of students working. One can start with the lighter book and one with the heavier one. If class time is available, have the teams switch books at the end. Otherwise, have them share data.
- Ideally, the values for maximum speed and momentum at impact should be the same for the two books because the release points are identical. This rarely happens, but these values should be close to each other if the data are acceptable.

Background Information

The momentum of a vehicle depends upon the mass of the vehicle and its velocity. The equation is $p = m \cdot v$, where p is the momentum, m is the mass, and v is the velocity.

If you make several assumptions, the distance that an object slides when it is hit by a moving object should be related to the square of the velocity, rather than to the velocity in the linear relationship modeled here. If students were able to make extremely accurate measurements of sliding distance and velocity, they would see the square relationship. However, because the books tend to slide in different directions and accurate velocity measurements are difficult to obtain, the students will probably see a linear, rather than a square, relationship. You may want to discuss this with your students.

Modifications

If time is short, have students skip step 17.

Sample Data

Weight of vehicle   <u>2.156 N</u>
Mass of vehicle   <u>0.220 kg</u>

For the Heavy Book

Weight of book   <u>6.407 N</u>
Mass of book   <u>0.654 kg</u>

Distance Vehicle Traveled Before Colliding with Book (m)	Average Velocity of Vehicle (m/sec)	Average Distance Book Moved (m)	Average Momentum of Vehicle at Impact (kg·m/sec)
0.8	2.336	0.1	0.514
0.7	2.040	0.09	0.449
0.5	1.717	0.068	0.378
0.35	1.551	0.048	0.341
0.25	1.243	0.030	0.273

```
LinReg
  y=ax+b
  a=.3048509377
  b=-.0519967166
  r²=.9736877776
  r=.9867561895
```

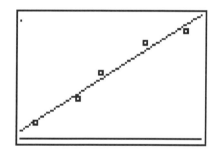

For the Light Book

Weight of book   <u>5.2828 N</u>
Mass of book   <u>0.483   kg</u>

Distance Vehicle Traveled Before Colliding with Book (m)	Average Velocity of Vehicle (m/sec)	Average Distance Book Moved (m)	Average Momentum of Vehicle at Impact (kg·m/sec)
0.8	2.201	0.14	0.484
0.7	2.074	0.124	0.456
0.5	1.652	0.081	0.363
0.35	1.438	0.064	0.316
0.25	1.285	0.040	0.283

```
LinReg
 y=ax+b
 a=.4756065453
 b=-.0911207298
 r²=.9942686652
 r=.9971302148
■
```

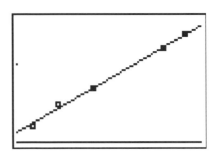

Case Analysis Answers

1. Is the linear regression a good fit to the data for the heavy book? For the light book? Explain.
   Since r and r² are close to 1, a linear relationship between momentum and distance is a good model for the data. For the sample data, the data for the light book are better than those for the heavy book.

2. For the *heavy* book, write the equation for the distance vs. momentum graph. Use $y = ax + b$ and values from step 25. The y is distance the book moved, and x is momentum at impact.
   Answers will vary. For the sample data, the equation is y = 0.305x ⁻0.052.

3. Using your equation, calculate how far the book would move if its momentum at impact were 0.7 kg·m/sec. Show your work. Don't forget that your answer has units.
   Answers will vary. For the sample data, y = 0.305 × 0.7 ⁻0.052 = 0.162 m, so the book would move 0.162 m.

4. If the book moved 0.2 m after impact, what would the momentum of the vehicle have been when it hit the book? Show your work.
   Distance = 0.20 = 0.305x ⁻0.052, so the momentum would be 0.826 kg·m/s.

5. Repeat questions 3 and 4 for the *light* book.
   Answers will vary. For the sample data, y = 0.476 × 0.7 ⁻0.091 = 0.242 m, so the book would move 0.242 m; if distance = 0.20 = 0.476x ⁻0.091, the momentum would be 0.611 kg·m/s.

6. The equation for the accident scene is $y = 0.00245x$ ⁻37.8, where y is distance the van moved (in meters) and x is momentum of the car at impact (in kg·m/s). What was the car's momentum just before it hit the van? (Hint: Rearrange the equation to solve for x.) Show your work.
   y =1.6 = 0.00245x ⁻37.8
   39.4 = 0.00245x
   momentum, x = 16,082 kg·m/s

7. What was the impact velocity of the car in meters per second? Show your work. (Hint: Rearrange the momentum equation, $p = m·v$ where p is momentum, m is mass, and v is velocity. Then substitute for momentum, from question 6, and mass of the car, 1000 kg.)
   momentum = 16,082 = 1000v
   velocity, v = 16.08 m/s

8. If the speed limit on the road was 50 mph, was the car speeding just before it hit the van? Show your work. (Hint: Multiply velocity in meters per second, from the last question, by 2.24.)
   velocity, v = 16.08 × 2.24 = 36.0
   The car was not speeding because its velocity at impact was 36.0 mph.

Case File 7

Drug Tests: Identifying an unknown chemical

Use quantitative and qualitative analyses to identify the powder in Mr. Orlow's car.

Police Report

Patrol officers pulled over Mr. Yuri Orlow for reckless driving last night at 8:50 p.m. A preliminary Breathalyzer test showed that Mr. Orlow was intoxicated. Mr. Orlow consented to a search of the vehicle, in which the officers found traces of a white powder that seemed to have leaked across the leather of the passenger seat. The officers think that Mr. Orlow might have thrown a bag of the unknown substance out the open passenger-side window before pulling over. A search of the snowy road has revealed nothing. The powder has been sent to the lab for testing.

Mr. Orlow has been charged with driving recklessly and awaits a second charge pending the results of the tests on the white powder.

Enclosed are two photographs of Mr. Orlow's car and an evidence vial containing a sample of the powder.

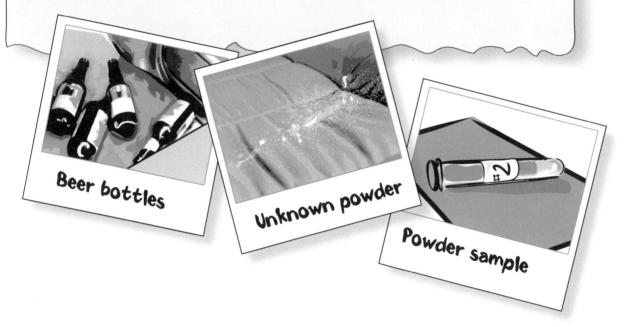

Beer bottles

Unknown powder

Powder sample

Forensics Objective

- identify an unknown powder using physical and chemical properties

Science and Mathematics Objectives

- distinguish between physical and chemical properties
- distinguish between qualitative and quantitative observation

Materials (for each group)

- TI-83/TI-84 Plus™ Family
- Vernier EasyData™ application
- Vernier EasyLink™
- pH Sensor
- Conductivity Probe
- vinegar
- 5 known and 1 unknown "drug" samples (4 g of each)
- distilled or deionized water
- spoons and/or weighing paper (one per sample)
- filter paper
- six 50 mL beakers
- stirring rod
- disposable pipettes or droppers
- wash bottle (with deionized water)
- magnifying glass
- balance
- lint-free tissues
- goggles (1 pair per student)

Procedure

Caution: Obtain and wear goggles during this experiment. Avoid inhaling the powders. Do not taste or smell any of the powders. If you get any powder or liquid on your skin, wash it with water immediately. Tell your teacher right away if any spills or accidents occur.

Part I: Appearance ● ● ●

1. Label five 50 mL beakers with numbers 1 through 5. Label one beaker "Unknown" for the powder taken from Mr. Orlow's car. Using the balance, measure 2 g of each sample and place it in the proper beaker. (To avoid cross-contamination of the other samples, use a different weighing paper or spoon for each sample. Save the spoons or weighing papers for use in Part V.)

2. Observe the samples through the magnifying glass, and record your observations in the Evidence Record.

Part II: Preparing the Solutions ● ● ●

3. Prepare powder-and-water mixtures of the six samples.
   a) Add 20 mL distilled or deionized water to each beaker prepared in step 1. Stir the mixtures thoroughly with the stirring rod. (Note: After stirring one sample, rinse the stirring rod with deionized water and dry it with a lint-free tissue before using it to mix another sample.)
   b) Stir each mixture once every 3 minutes for 15 minutes. After the final stir, let the mixtures settle for about 5 minutes.

c)   Write any observations that you can make about the water mixtures into the Evidence Record. (Did they fizz? Were the powders very soluble, or not soluble at all?)

Part III: Testing the pH of the Samples ● ● ●

4.   Connect the EasyLink to the USB port in your calculator. Then connect a pH Sensor to the port on the EasyLink. (Note: For this experiment, your teacher already has the pH Sensor in a pH soaking solution in a beaker. Be careful not to tip over the beaker when you connect the sensor to the interface.)

5.   Set up the EasyData App for data collection.
   a)   Select ⌈File⌉ from the Main screen.
   b)   Select option **1: New** to reset the application. The Main screen should be displayed. The Main screen displays the current reading from the pH probe.

> At the bottom of the Main screen are five options (⌈File⌉, ⌈Setup⌉, ⌈Start⌉, ⌈Graph⌉, and ⌈Quit⌉). Each of these options can be selected by pressing the calculator key located below it (⌐Y=⌐, ⌐WINDOW⌐, ⌐ZOOM⌐, ⌐TRACE⌐, or ⌐GRAPH⌐).

6.   Use the pH Sensor to determine the pH of the solution in each sample beaker.
   a)   Rinse the tip of the pH Sensor with deionized water from the wash bottle and place it into the liquid in the beaker containing sample 1. Be careful not to let the tip of the sensor touch any solid material at the bottom of the beaker.
   b)   When the pH reading on the Main screen has stabilized, record it in the Evidence Record.
   c)   Repeat steps 6a and 6b for each of the remaining samples.

7.   When you are finished, rinse the pH Sensor with deionized water and return it to its storage container.

Part IV: Testing the Conductivity of the Samples ● ● ●

8.   Disconnect the pH Sensor from the EasyLink.

9.   Connect the Conductivity Probe to the EasyLink. Set the switch on the probe to the 0–20,000 μS setting.

10. Select ⌈File⌉ from the Main screen, and then select option **1: New** to reset the application.

11. Zero the Conductivity Probe.
   a)   Place the probe in a beaker of deionized water. Select ⌈Setup⌉.
   b)   Select option **7: Zero**. On the resulting screen, select ⌈Zero⌉.

12. Collect conductivity data for each sample.
   a)   Place the tip of the probe into the liquid in the beaker containing sample 1. The hole near the tip of the probe should be completely covered by the liquid.
   b)   When the conductivity reading on the Main screen has stabilized, record it in your Evidence Record.
   c)   Rinse the Conductivity Probe thoroughly with deionized water from the wash bottle before collecting data for the next sample.
   d)   Repeat steps 12a–12c for each of the remaining samples.

13. Empty the remaining liquid from the beakers as directed by your teacher. Rinse and dry the beakers.

Part V: Reaction of the Samples with Vinegar

14. In the next test, you will observe the reaction of each of the samples with vinegar, an acid.
    a) Using the balance, measure 2 g of each sample and put it in the proper beaker. (To avoid cross-contamination of the samples, use the measuring papers or spoons that you used in step 1 or use a new paper or clean spoon for each sample.)
    b) Add 10 mL of vinegar to each sample. Observe what reaction takes place (if any). Record your observations in the Evidence Record.

15. When you have observed and recorded the reactions of all of the samples with vinegar, then empty, rinse, and dry the beakers as directed by your teacher.

Name: _____

Date: _____

Evidence Record

Sample	General Appearance	Observations of Water Mixture	pH	Conductivity (µS/cm)	Reaction with Vinegar
1					
2					
3					
4					
5					
Unknown					

Case Analysis

1. Based on your observations, which known sample do you think was most similar to the unknown powder found in Mr. Orlow's car? Do you think the unknown was an exact match to that known sample? Explain your answer.
2. Why was it important to measure the amounts of the substances that you used in the lab?
3. Explain the difference between physical and chemical properties. Give two examples of physical properties and one example of a chemical property that you measured in the lab.
4. Explain the difference between qualitative and quantitative observations. Give one example of a qualitative observation and one example of a quantitative observation that you made in the lab.
5. Identify two tests, other than those that you carried out in this investigation, that forensic scientists can use to identify a suspected drug.

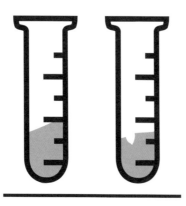

Case File 7
Drug Tests: Identifying an unknown chemical

Teacher Notes

Teaching time: one or two class periods

This lab uses the identification of an unknown "drug" to demonstrate the differences between chemical and physical properties and between qualitative and quantitative observations.

Tips

If pH or conductivity readings do not stabilize, have students collect data in Single Point mode (from the Main screen, select [Setup] and then option **5: Single Point**). When the students select [Start], the probe or sensor will collect data for 10 seconds and then display an average reading on the screen.

Lab Preparation

- The following powders work well as samples and unknowns: flour, powdered (ground) salt (NaCl), powdered sugar ($C_6H_{12}O_6$), baking powder ($NaAl(SO_4)_2$ or $NaHCO_3 + KHC_4H_4O_6$), baking soda ($NaHCO_3$), talcum powder, baby formula, plaster of paris ($CaSO_4 \cdot \frac{1}{2}H_2O$), cornstarch ($C_6H_{10}O_5$), chalk ($CaCO_3$), and Epsom salts ($MgSO_4 \cdot 7H_2O$).
- You can use empty 35 mm film canisters or other small containers to distribute the unknowns. The lab will go faster if the correct amount of each sample is measured beforehand and given to each group.

Resources

Although the powders being tested in this lab are not illegal drugs, the procedures used by the students are similar to some used by professional forensic chemists. The sites listed below provide information about procedures and techniques for the identification of real drugs.

http://www.swgdrug.org/approved.htm
This site of the Scientific Working Group for the Analysis of Seized Drugs provides information about processes and procedures that are used in the analysis and identification of unknown (presumably illegal) drugs.

http://chrom.tutms.tut.ac.jp/JINNO/DRUGDATA/00database.html
This extensive database of prescription and nonprescription drugs, organized alphabetically or by drug classification (such as analgesic or antipsychotic), provides chemical composition and structure, physical properties, and analytical results.

http://www.streetdrugs.org/index.htm
This comprehensive Web site discusses characteristics, sources, and effects of various street drugs.

Modifications

If you wish, you can use this activity to introduce or explain heats of reaction to your students. Several of the possible "drugs" will show measurable temperature changes when they react with or dissolve in water or vinegar. Have the students measure the temperatures of the water and the vinegar before they are added to the solids in steps 3 and 14. Have them continue to measure the temperatures as the various powders are added and dissolve in and/or react with the liquids. You can have the students use the Vernier EasyTemp™ temperature probe to monitor the temperatures. This will require *either* that you provide one calculator and temperature probe for each mixture (six per group) *or* that you have the students mix the solutions and measure the temperatures one at a time (requiring more than 90 minutes if the temperature of each mixture is recorded for 15 minutes). If you have a limited number of calculators or time is short, it may be better to have the students use traditional thermometers to monitor the temperatures.

Sample Data

Sample	General Appearance	Observations of Water Mixture	pH	Conductivity (µS/cm)	Reaction with Vinegar
1 (Flour)	Fine, white powder	Did not dissolve	6.5	345	Did not react
2 (Baking Soda)	Fine, white powder	Partially dissolved	8.0	1.39E4	Fizzed vigorously
3 (Baking Powder)	Fine, white powder	Fizzed vigorously	6.9	9049	Fizzed vigorously
4 (Salt)	Fine, white powder	Dissolved	6.7	1.76E4	Nearly dissolved
5 (Sugar)	Fine, white powder	Dissolved	7.2	0	Nearly dissolved
Unknown	Fine, white powder	Fizzed vigorously	6.5	9263	Fizzed vigorously

Case Analysis Answers

1. Based on your observations, which known sample do you think was most similar to the unknown powder found in Mr. Orlow's car? Do you think the unknown was an exact match to that known sample? Explain your answer.
   Answers will vary. Students should describe what properties led to the choice for the unknown. For the sample data, Mr. Orlow's powder appears to be baking powder (with similar pH, conductivity, and reactions with water and vinegar).
2. Why was it important to measure the amounts of the substances that you used in the lab?
   When making comparisons, you must keep all untested variables constant.
3. Explain the difference between physical and chemical properties. Give two examples of physical properties and one example of a chemical property that you measured in the lab.
   Physical properties are properties that you can measure without changing the substance. When chemical properties are measured, the substance is destroyed. The physical properties measured here included solubility, pH, and conductivity. The chemical properties measured were the reactions with water and vinegar.
4. Explain the difference between qualitative and quantitative observations. Give one example of a qualitative observation and one example of a quantitative observation that you made in the lab.
   In a qualitative observation of a substance, you use one of the five senses without taking a measurement. A quantitative observation requires a numerical measurement of some property of the substance. Qualitative observations included dissolution or no dissolution in water and reactions with water and vinegar. Quantitative observations included pH and conductivity.
5. Identify two tests, other than those that you carried out in this investigation, that forensic scientists can use to identify a suspected drug.
   Forensic scientists can use gas chromatography (GC), mass spectroscopy (MS), infrared spectroscopy (FTIR), column chromatography, electrophoresis, titration, precipitation reactions, redox reactions, and other chemical reactions.

Case File 8

No Dumping:
Using soil characteristics to link suspects to a crime scene

Use physical and chemical characteristics of soils to identify a soil sample from a certain area.

Police Report

Early Saturday morning, two local teenagers called police after observing a large, dark blue pickup truck dumping toxic materials in City Park. Due to the dim morning light, the boys were unable to see a license plate number. They did, however, recognize the make and model of the pickup truck. Police quickly apprehended four suspects who drive trucks of this make and model.

All four suspects deny having been anywhere near City Park in recent weeks.

Although tire tracks were found at the scene, the tread patterns were smudged. No toxic residue was found in the payloads of any of the trucks, but police were able to collect soil samples from underneath the bumpers.

Police suspect that an organized crime network is illegally dumping toxic material in exchange for large payoffs from local chemical company ZenCorp. We must identify the perpetrators in order to crack this ring.

Dump site at City Park Suspect 1 rear bumper Suspect 2 rear bumper Suspect 3 rear bumper Suspect 4 rear bumper

Forensics Objective

- identify characteristics of different soils to demonstrate that a suspect has been at a scene

Science and Mathematics Objectives

- use characteristic properties to identify a sample
- measure the pH of soils
- measure the water absorbency of soils
- measure the conductivity of soils

Materials (for each group)

- TI-83/TI-84 Plus™ Family
- Vernier EasyData™ application
- Vernier EasyLink™
- pH Sensor
- Conductivity Probe
- magnifying glass
- coarse filter papers (12.5 cm diameter)
- distilled or deionized water
- lint-free tissues
- wash bottle (with deionized water)
- 100 mL graduated cylinder
- five 250 mL beakers
- 5 spoons or weighing papers
- 400 mL beaker
- 50 mL beaker for deionized water
- stirring rod
- funnel large enough for 50 g of soil and 100 mL of water
- balance
- 100 g each of soil samples for 4 suspects and 1 crime scene
- goggles (1 pair per student)

Procedure

Part I: Preparing the Soil-and-Water Mixtures ● ● ●

Caution: Obtain and wear goggles during this experiment. Tell your teacher right away in case of any spills or accidents.

1. Prepare mixtures of water and soil. For each sample, complete the following steps:
   a) Label a 250 mL beaker with the sample number.
   b) Using a balance, measure 50 g of the soil sample and place it in the labeled beaker. (Note: To avoid contaminating the other samples, use a different spoon or weighing paper for each sample.)
   c) Measure 100 mL of distilled or deionized water in the graduated cylinder. Add the water to the soil in the beaker.
   d) Stir the mixture thoroughly with the stirring rod.
   e) Stir the mixture once every 3 minutes for 15 minutes.
   f) After the final stir, let the mixture settle for 5 minutes before beginning to take readings. (Note: To avoid contaminating the other samples, rinse the stirring rod with deionized water between soil samples.)

Part II: Measuring the pH of the Samples ● ● ●

2. Connect EasyLink to the USB port in your calculator. Then connect the pH Sensor to the port on the EasyLink. (Note: Your teacher already has the pH Sensor in a pH soaking solution in a beaker. Be careful not to tip over the beaker when you connect the sensor to the interface.)

3. Set up the EasyData App for data collection.
   a)   Select [File] from the Main screen.
   b)   Select option **1: New** to reset the application. The Main screen should be displayed. The Main screen displays the current reading from the pH Sensor.

At the bottom of the Main screen are five options ([File], [Setup], [Start], [Graph], and [Quit]). Each of these options can be selected by pressing the calculator key located below it (Y= , WINDOW , ZOOM , TRACE , or GRAPH).

---

4. Use the pH Sensor to determine the pH of the solution in each sample beaker.
   a)   Rinse the tip of the pH Sensor with deionized water from the wash bottle, and place it into the liquid in the beaker for sample 1. Be careful not to let the tip of the sensor touch any solid material at the bottom of the beaker.
   b)   When the pH reading on the Main screen has stabilized, record the pH of the solution in the Evidence Record.
   c)   Repeat steps 4a and 4b for each remaining soil sample. When you are finished, rinse the pH Sensor with deionized water and return it to its storage container.

Part III: Testing the Conductivity of the Samples ● ● ●

5. Replace the pH Sensor connected to EasyLink with the Conductivity Probe. Set the switch on the probe to the 0–20,000 µS setting.

6. Select [File] from the Main screen, and then select option **1: New** to reset the application.

7. Zero the Conductivity Probe.
   a)   Place the probe in a beaker of deionized water. Select [Setup].
   b)   Select option **7: Zero**. On the resulting screen, select [Zero].

8. Collect conductivity data for each of the samples.
   a)   Place the tip of the probe into the liquid in the beaker for sample 1. The hole near the tip of the probe should be completely covered by the liquid. Be careful not to disturb any solid material remaining at the bottom of the beaker.
   b)   When the conductivity reading has stabilized, record the conductivity of the solution in the Evidence Record.
   c)   Rinse the conductivity probe thoroughly with deionized water from the wash bottle.
   d)   Repeat steps 8a–8c for each of the remaining samples.

Part IV: The Physical Appearance of the Samples ● ● ●

9. For each sample, use the balance to measure out 50 g on a piece of filter paper labeled with the sample number.

10. Examine the samples through the magnifying glass. In the Evidence Record, make a sketch of each sample and write down some notes about its appearance.

Part V: Determining the Water Absorbency of the Samples ● ● ●

11. Determine how well each sample absorbs water.
   a)   Carefully lift the sample 1 filter paper and soil that you prepared in step 9.
   b)   Place the filter paper and soil into a funnel.

---

c) Have your lab partner hold the funnel over a 400 mL beaker.

d) Measure 100 mL of deionized water in the graduated cylinder, and pour it through the soil. Collect any water that drains through in the beaker.

e) Let the sample drip for 60 seconds.

f) Pour the water from the beaker into the 100 mL graduated cylinder.

g) Subtract the volume of water in the graduated cylinder from the 100 mL you poured into the soil. This is the amount of water absorbed by the soil. Write this amount in the Water Absorbency column of your Evidence Record.

h) For each remaining soil sample, empty the funnel, 400 mL beaker, and graduated cylinder and repeat steps 11a–11g.

Name: _____

Date: _____

Evidence Record

Sample	pH	Conductivity (μS/cm)	Water Absorbency (mL/50 g)	General Appearance
Sample 1				
Sample 2				
Sample 3				
Sample 4				
Crime Scene				

Sketch of Physical Appearance

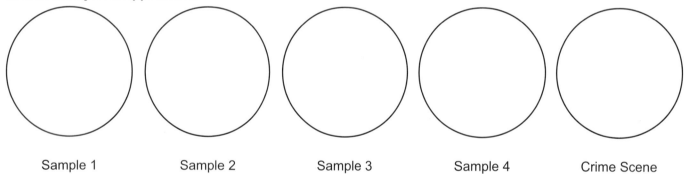

Sample 1   Sample 2   Sample 3   Sample 4   Crime Scene

Case Analysis

1. What is the range of pH that you found in the five soil samples?
2. What does a high pH mean, and what does a low pH mean?
3. What can cause a soil to become acidic or basic?
4. What is the range of conductivity that you found?
5. What does a high conductivity indicate about the soil?
6. Why is it important to know the pH *and* the conductivity of a soil if you want to know how salty the soil is?
7. What is the range of water absorbency that you found?
8. What types of soils have a high water absorbency, and what types of soils have a low water absorbency?
9. How can an investigator use the physical appearance of a soil sample to link a suspect to a victim or crime scene?
10. What tools can a forensic scientist use to identify and match soil samples?
11. Based on your observations, were any of the suspects' vehicles present at the crime scene? If so, which ones? Explain your answer.

Case File 8
No Dumping:
Using soil characteristics to link suspects to a crime scene

Teacher Notes

Teaching time: two class periods

This lab introduces students to the importance of soils and other trace evidence in connecting victims, crime scenes, and suspects.

Tips

- To save class time, weigh out soil samples for the students before class.
- Before assigning this activity, you may want to review characteristics of soils and the concepts of pH, conductivity, and water absorbency (see Background Information).
- If you have access to a microscope that is connected to a computer, you can have students print out micrographs of the soil samples and label them to show matching features.
- If pH or conductivity readings do not stabilize, have students collect data in Single Point mode (from the Main screen, select [Setup] and then option **5: Single Point**). When the students select [Start], the probe or sensor will collect data for 10 seconds and then display an average reading on the screen.

Lab Preparation

- For the samples, you can either use soils from several different sources or develop samples by mixing materials yourself. If you use soils from different sources, the differences in appearance will probably be significant. If you make the samples artificially, the students will have to rely more heavily on the chemical tests to match a sample to the crime scene.
- Different soils can be made with a variety of materials, including potting soils, compost, topsoil, clay, sand, lime, mud, and peat moss.
- To make soil samples that look similar, start with one soil sample and add different chemicals to it to create several different samples. Wetting the soil with a little weak sodium hydroxide (100 mL of 1 M aqueous NaOH to 500 g of soil) will create an alkaline soil. Similarly, wetting soil with a little weak hydrochloric acid (100 mL of 1 M aqueous HCl to 500 g of soil) will make it acidic. You can also add 100 mL of 1 M aqueous sodium chloride to 500 g of soil to increase the salinity without changing the pH. Sand or peat moss can be added to change water absorbency. Mix each sample well to ensure that it is uniform. Make sure the soil is dry before lab day.

Background Information

Soil is made up of tiny particles of rock, mineral grains, and organic matter. The sources of these materials and the quantity of each of them make a particular soil unique. These materials also affect the pH, conductivity, particle size, and water absorbency of the soil. Because soils are unique, matching characteristics from soil samples can help to place a victim or suspect at a particular location.

In many cases, the physical appearance of a soil, including the distinct rock types and plant matter present, can allow a forensic geologist to place someone at a crime scene with a high degree of certainty. The physical appearance of soils in many areas changes over time. For example, the soils along the banks of rivers can change from month to month as water levels fluctuate. In areas with frequent changes, soil matching can sometimes allow investigators to determine even the *time* someone was in a location.

Conductivity (salinity)

Soil conductivity is a measure of how well a soil conducts electricity. Ions in the soil make it conductive, so conductivity is a measurement of the ions present. Because salts produce highly conductive ions, the conductivity of a soil is often referred to as its *salinity*. However, most ions—including hydronium (H_3O^+) and hydroxide (OH^-) ions—can increase the conductivity of the soil, so a soil with a high conductivity is not necessarily extremely salty. By examining both conductivity and pH, you can determine whether a soil has a high salt concentration.

Conductive ions can be introduced to soils by the natural weathering of minerals, irrigation, or runoff from salted roads. Poor drainage and hot, dry weather also contribute to the buildup of salt in the soil. Sodium chloride, NaCl, is the most common salt found, but others, such as calcium chloride ($CaCl_2$) and magnesium sulfate ($MgSO_4$), are often present as well.

Conductivity is measured in the unit *siemens* (S) per meter or centimeter ($1\ S = 1\ kg^{-1} \cdot m^{-2} \cdot s^3 \cdot A^2$). In this lab, conductivities are measured in microsiemens per centimeter (µS/cm), although the probe is labeled simply "µS."

pH

pH is a measure of how acidic or basic a substance is. A substance with a low pH (below 7) is considered acidic, while a substance with a high pH (above 7) is considered basic, or alkaline. A pH of 7 is neutral. The pH of a soil is related to its composition. Soils with large amounts of organic matter tend to be more acidic than soils without organic matter. Some types of minerals can affect a soil's pH if they dissolve in water. For example, calcite ($CaCO_3$) can produce a basic solution when it dissolves. The pH of a soil can be affected by human and environmental factors also, such as acid rain and fertilizer application.

Water absorbency

Soils can absorb different amounts of water, depending on their composition. Generally speaking, soils that are made of small particles, such as silt, tend to be able to absorb more water than soils made of larger particles, such as sand. The chemical composition of the particles also affects how absorbent a soil is; clay particles tend to have charged surfaces, so they are more attractive to water and more absorbent than other types of minerals. Organic matter can substantially increase a soil's water-absorbing capacity.

Color

The color of a soil is determined by its composition. Soils with much organic matter in them tend to be dark brown or black. The mineral and rock particles that make up the soil often give soils characteristic colors. For example, the iron-rich mud of the southern United States is red.

Resources

http://cals.arizona.edu/pubs/garden/mg/soils/index.html
The online *Arizona Master Gardener Manual* from the University of Arizona Cooperative Extension provides information on the many different types of soils and their characteristics.

http://www.interpol.int/Public/Forensic/IFSS/meeting13/Reviews/Soil.pdf
This Web site contains notes and summaries of soil identification methods from an international forensic science symposium.

Modifications

- For less-advanced students, the number of tests that are carried out on each sample can be reduced. You can also make the samples less similar in appearance or properties.
- For more-advanced students, you can combine different soil types to make the matching process more difficult. More than four suspect samples can be used. Students can also be encouraged to explore the processes of soil identification and analysis in more detail.

Sample Data

Sample	pH	Conductivity (µS/cm)	Water Absorbency (mL/50 g)	General Appearance
Sample 1 (Topsoil)	7.0	1338	35	Fine particles, small lumps, silvery specks
Sample 2 (Topsoil with HCl)	5.8	3462	20	Fine particles, small lumps, silvery specks
Sample 3 (Topsoil with NaCl)	7.3	4571	25	Fine particles, small lumps, silvery specks
Sample 4 (Topsoil with NaOH)	9.8	2966	28	Fine particles, small lumps, silvery specks
Crime Scene	7.1	4358	23	Fine particles, small lumps, silvery specks

Case Analysis Answers

1. What is the range of pH that you found in the five soil samples?
   Answers will vary. For the sample data, pH ranged from 5.8 to 9.8.
2. What does a high pH mean, and what does a low pH mean?
   High pH means basic, or alkaline, soil; low pH means acidic soil.
3. What can cause a soil to become acidic or basic?
   Mineral composition, the presence of organic matter, and environmental factors can change the pH of a soil.
4. What is the range of conductivity that you found?
   Answers will vary. For the sample data, conductivity ranged from 1338 to 4571 µS/cm.
5. What does a high conductivity indicate about the soil?
   There are many ions in the soil.

6. Why is it important to know the pH and the conductivity of a soil if you want to know how salty the soil is?

   Acids and bases can raise conductivity but will also change pH. A soil with a high conductivity and neutral pH is more likely to be salty than one with a high conductivity and extremely high or low pH.

7. What is the range of water absorbency that you found?

   Answers will vary. For the sample data, soils absorbed 20–35 mL water per 50 g sample.

8. What types of soils have high water absorbency, and what types of soils have low water absorbency?

   In general, soils with small particles and/or high levels of plant materials like sphagnum moss are highly absorbent. Sand and any nonporous soil with large particles will have low absorbency.

9. How can an investigator use the physical appearance of a soil sample to link a suspect or victim to a crime scene?

   If the soil has a distinctive color or mineral makeup, then investigators can use that characteristic to match a sample from the crime scene to a sample from a suspect or victim and show that the person was at the crime scene.

10. What tools do forensic scientists use to identify and match soil samples?

    They can use microscopes, pH meters, conductivity probes, magnifying glasses, mass spectrometers, ion probes, and chemical tests.

11. Based on your observations, were any of the suspects' vehicles present at the crime scene? If so, which ones? Explain your answer.

    Answers will vary. In the case of the sample data, sample 3 seems to match the crime scene: It has similar values for pH, absorbency, and conductivity, and it is similar in appearance.

Killer Cup of Coffee:
Using colorimetry to determine concentration of a poison

Determine the concentration of cyanide in the solution.

A Killer Cup of Coffee? GlobalTech Manager Dies

SOUTH PAINTER, Tuesday: It was a normal Monday morning at GlobalTech Industries until the mail boy discovered project manager Patrick Marchand dead in his cubicle, head on his desk. Mr. Marchand had died while writing an email, in a room full of people hard at work. An early examination of the crime scene yielded no clues.

Mr. Marchand was known to have a serious heart condition, and many signs pointed to cardiac arrest as the cause of his death. However, as police canvassed the office space, the distinct odor of bitter almonds was detected, and a vial containing a small amount of an unknown chemical was found discarded in a communal trash can.

Based on the bitter almond odor, police have tentatively identified the substance as cyanide. The existence of this possible poison has lead police to suspect foul play in Mr. Marchand's death. The police have no leads.

continued on p. D2

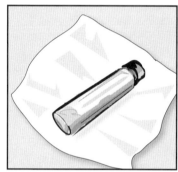

This vial, wrapped in a piece of tissue, was discovered in the bottom of a communal trash can near the GlobalTech office bathroom. It once contained an unspecified amount of cyanide.

LAB NOTES

Technician: Beverly Chin

-received vial containing 20 mL cyanide solution—concentration unknown

-reacted cyanide (CN^-) solution with potassium polysulfide (K_2S_x) to produce potassium thiocyanate (KSCN)

-reacted KSCN solution with iron(III)chloride ($FeCl_3$) to produce iron(III)thiocyanate ion ($FeSCN^{2+}$)

-determination of amount of $FeSCN^{2+}$ in reacted solution will allow estimation of concentration of CN^- in original solution

-included in package: $FeSCN^{2+}$ solution of unknown concentration

Forensics Objective

- use Beer's law to determine the concentration of iron(III)thiocyanate ($FeSCN^{2+}$) in an unknown solution

Science and Mathematics Objectives

- use colorimetry to determine the concentration of a colored species in a solution
- use a linear relationship to model Beer's law
- learn the importance of carefully prepared standards

Materials (for each group)

- TI-83/TI-84 Plus™ Family
- Vernier EasyData™ application
- Vernier EasyLink™
- Colorimeter
- 7 cuvettes
- colored wax pencil
- distilled or deionized water
- 50 mL of 0.15 M stock $FeSCN^{2+}$ solution
- 5 mL of $FeSCN^{2+}$ solution with unknown concentration
- two 10 mL pipettes or graduated cylinders
- two 50 mL beakers
- 5 stirring rods
- 2 droppers
- 5 test tubes
- test-tube rack
- lint-free tissues
- waste beaker
- goggles (1 pair per student)

Procedure

Part I: Preparing the Solutions ● ● ●

Goggles must be worn at all times during this lab activity! CAUTION: Be careful not to ingest any solutions or spill any on your skin. Inform your teacher immediately in the event of an accident.

1. Obtain all the solutions and label them with a wax pencil.
   a) Pour 50 mL of stock 0.15 M $FeSCN^{2+}$ solution into a 50 mL beaker. Label the beaker "0.15 M $FeSCN^{2+}$."
   b) Pour 30 mL of deionized or distilled water into a 50 mL beaker. Label the beaker "H_2O."

2. Prepare the standard solutions.
   a) Label five clean, dry test tubes with numbers 1 through 5.
   b) The table below shows how much water and stock $FeSCN^{2+}$ solution to add to each test tube. Use a pipette or a dropper and graduated cylinder to measure the correct amount of $FeSCN^{2+}$ solution into each test tube. (Note: Use a separate pipette or graduated cylinder and dropper for the water and the $FeSCN^{2+}$.)

Test Tube	FeSCN²⁺ Solution (mL)	Distilled Water (mL)	Final Concentration of FeSCN²⁺ (mol/L)
1	10	0	0.15
2	8	2	0.12
3	6	4	0.09
4	4	6	0.06
5	2	8	0.03

c) Carefully stir the contents of each test tube with a clean stirring rod. (Note: Use a separate rod for each test tube *or* carefully clean the stirring rod with deionized water and dry it with a tissue before using it in the next test tube.)

3. Prepare the blank, the five standard solutions, and the unknown for colorimetry. Use deionized water as the blank; use solutions from the five test tubes as standards.
   a) For each standard solution, rinse an empty cuvette twice with about 1 mL of the sample; do the same with deionized water for the blank.
   b) Fill the cuvette three-fourths full with the sample, and seal it with a lid.
   c) Label the lid with the sample number, "B" for the blank, or "?" for the unknown.
   d) Wipe the outside of the cuvette with a tissue.

   Remember the following:
   - All cuvettes should be clean and dry on the outside.
   - Handle a cuvette only by the top edge or the ribbed sides.
   - All solutions should be free of bubbles.
   - Label the *lid* of the cuvette so the label does not interfere with the beam of light.

Part II: Collecting the Data ●●●

4. Connect the Colorimeter to EasyLink. Connect EasyLink to the USB port on the calculator. The EasyData application should start automatically.

5. Set up the EasyData App to collect absorbance readings.
   a) Select (File) from the Main screen, and then select option **1: New** to reset the application.
   b) Select (Setup) from the Main screen, and then select option **3: Events with Entry**.

6. Calibrate the Colorimeter.
   a) Place the blank in the cuvette slot of the Colorimeter. Make sure that one of the transparent faces of the cuvette is pointing toward the white reference mark. Close the lid of the Colorimeter.
   b) Set the wavelength on the Colorimeter to 470 nm. This will set the Colorimeter's light emitter and receiver to emit and record blue light.
   c) Calibrate by pressing the CAL button on the Colorimeter.
   d) When the red light on the Colorimeter stops flashing, remove the cuvette from the Colorimeter.

7. You are now ready to collect absorbance data for the five standard solutions.
   a) Place cuvette 1 into the Colorimeter and close the lid.
   b) Select (Start) to begin data collection.
   c) When the value displayed on the calculator screen has stabilized, select (Keep) to record the absorbance of the first standard.
   d) The calculator will ask you to enter a value. Enter the concentration of FeSCN²⁺ in the solution (from the table in step 2). Select (OK) to store this absorbance-concentration data pair.

e) Repeat steps 7a–7d for each of the remaining standards. Be sure to enter the correct concentration for each standard in step 7d.

8. Select ⌈Stop⌉ when you have finished collecting data for all the standards.

9. EasyData should display a graph showing concentration of $FeSCN^{2+}$ on the *x*-axis and absorbance of blue light on the *y*-axis. Examine the data points on the displayed graph. As you move the cursor right or left with the arrow keys, the values for concentration, **X**, and absorbance, **Y**, for each data point are displayed above the graph. Write the absorbance value, rounded to the nearest 0.001, for each standard solution in your Evidence Record.

10. Select ⌈Main⌉ to return to the Main screen.

11. Place the cuvette with the unknown solution in the Colorimeter. Monitor the absorbance value displayed on the calculator. When this value has stabilized, round it to the nearest 0.001 and write it in your Evidence Record.

12. Discard the remaining solutions as directed by your teacher.

Part III: Analyzing the Data ● ● ●

13. To determine the concentration of $FeSCN^{2+}$ in the unknown solution, plot a graph of absorbance vs. concentration for your *standard* solutions and fit a straight line to the points. Then use the absorbance value of the unknown to estimate its concentration of $FeSCN^{2+}$.
    a) Select ⌈Graph⌉ from the Main screen.
    b) Select ⌈Anlyz⌉ from the graph screen, and then select **Linear Fit**. The equation for a straight line is $y = ax + b$, where y is absorbance, *x* is concentration, a is the slope, and b is the *y*-intercept. The screen will display the values of **a** and **b** that give the best fitting line to your data points. The correlation coefficient, **R**, indicates how well the data points match the regression line. A value of 1.00 indicates a perfect fit. Record the values of a, b, and *r* in the Evidence Record.
    c) To display the straight line on the graph of absorbance vs. concentration, select ⌈OK⌉. The line should closely fit the five data points and pass through, or near, the origin of the graph. The linear relationship between absorbance and concentration is known as Beer's law.
    d) The cursor is initially on the first data point. Press ⌂ to move from the data points to the line. The **X** and **Y** coordinates of the cursor will be shown on the screen above the graph. Use the arrow keys to move the cursor left and right along the line to the absorbance value, **Y**, that is closest to the absorbance reading you obtained for the unknown. The corresponding **X** value is the estimated concentration of $FeSCN^{2+}$ in the unknown solution. Write this value in the Evidence Record.

Name: _____

Date: _____

Evidence Record

Solution Number	Concentration of FeSCN^{2+} in Solution (mol/L)	Absorbance
1	0.15	
2	0.12	
3	0.09	
4	0.06	
5	0.03	
?	Unknown	

Concentration of FeSCN^{2+} in the unknown solution _____

y	ax + b
a	
b	
r	

Case Analysis

1. Write the equation for the line in the form $y = ax + b$, using the values for a and b that you recorded in the Evidence Record. For example, if a = 3 and b = 6, then the equation for the line is $y = 3x + 6$.

2. Use the equation to calculate the concentration of FeSCN^{2+} in the unknown solution. How does the value you calculate compare with the value you read from the graph?

3. The volume of the cyanide solution that was found at the scene was 20 mL. Based on the calculated concentration of FeSCN^{2+} in the unknown solution, determine the concentration of potassium cyanide, KCN, in the original poison. Show all your work. Give your answer in milligrams of KCN per milliliter of solution.
   (Hint: One mole of KCN will produce one mole of FeSCN^{2+}. Assume that all of the KCN in the poisoned solution reacted to form FeSCN^{2+}. Assume that the 20 mL of original solution was not diluted during the reaction to form FeSCN^{2+} and that the sample you received was also undiluted. The molecular weight of FeSCN^{2+} is 114 g/mol. The molecular weight of KCN is 65 g/mol.)

4. For most people, swallowing 300 mg of KCN is fatal. Based on the concentration of KCN in the poison that you calculated in question 3, determine the approximate volume of poison that the victim would have to have swallowed for it to have killed him. Show all your work.

5. Is it likely that the poison was the direct cause of death? Explain your answer. (Hint: Remember that the vial was mostly empty and may, at one time, have held more than 20 mL.)

6. Suppose you found out that the concentration of FeSCN^{2+} in the unknown was actually very different from the value you calculated in question 2 and the value you read off the graph. What factors could have caused that to happen?

Case File 9
Killer Cup of Coffee:
Using colorimetry to determine concentration of a poison

Teacher Notes

Teaching time: one class period

This lab introduces students to colorimetry. Students will calculate the concentration of an unknown by measuring how it absorbs a specific wavelength of light. The activity also demonstrates the importance of accurately made standard solutions.

Tips

- Use of the Colorimeter with the calculator is extremely battery intensive. Keep extra batteries on hand. Make sure that all solution preparation and cuvette filling is done *before* turning on the Colorimeter, in order to minimize the battery drain on the calculator.
- If class time is limited, prepare the solutions (Part I) for the students before class.
- Before assigning the activity, you may want to review the visible spectrum of light and the concept of light absorbance. In addition, you may want to discuss the chemistry involved in the reactions. (See Background Information below.)
- The concentration and type of dye, as well as the size of the drops, can vary in different brands of food coloring. You may need to test several brands of food coloring in order to get consistent results. The stock solution directions and sample data below were obtained when Durkee® red food coloring was used.

Lab Preparation

- You will be preparing a solution of red food coloring dissolved in water to simulate the cyanide-laced poison found at a crime scene. Food coloring is used so that preparation and disposal are easier, and safety issues with students handling the solutions are minimized.
- Prepare the simulated 0.50 M $FeSCN^{2+}$ stock solution by adding 2 drops of red food coloring to 100 mL of deionized water.
- To prepare the unknown so that the test will determine that it is lethal, mix 7 mL of the stock solution with 3 mL of deionized water. This will give an unknown concentration of about 0.105 M, which corresponds to a fatal dose of about 1.5 oz (equivalent to about three or four coffee creamers).
- To prepare the unknown so that the test will determine that it is not lethal, mix 1 mL of the stock solution with 9 mL of deionized water. This will give an unknown concentration of about 0.015 M, which corresponds to a fatal dose of about 10.4 oz. Although this is not a huge amount, it seems unlikely that anyone could have added that much solution to Mr. Marchand's coffee without his noticing.

Background Information

The primary objective of this experiment is to use a Colorimeter to determine the concentration of an unknown solution. In this device, blue light (470 nm) from the LED light source will pass through the solution and strike a photocell. A complementary color is used when a solution is tested in this way. We see the solution as a red color because the substances in the liquid are reflecting specific wavelengths of visible light and absorbing other wavelengths. Blue light is used in the test because the solution is absorbing those wavelengths, and the amount of blue light absorbed is proportional to the concentration of the substance in solution. A colored solution of higher concentration absorbs more light, and transmits less light, than a solution of lower concentration.

The reaction of the ferric ion (Fe3+) and thiocyanate ion (SCN–) produces the red brown solution simulated in this experiment. The table below shows the relationship between ion species and color.

$Fe^{3+}(aq)$	+	$SCN^-(aq) \rightarrow FeSCN^{2+}(aq)$	
yellow		colorless	red brown

Modifications

- For less-advanced students, prepare the standard solutions (Part I) in advance.
- For more-advanced students, use several different unknowns. More-advanced students may also benefit from using qualitative chemical components. You can create stock solutions of KSCN and $FeCl_3$ or $Fe(NO_3)_3$ and have the students carry out the reaction in the Background Information section. Please note that even low concentrations of these chemicals give intensely colored solutions that may not give linear results when blue light is used. You may have to use very dilute solutions in order to get usable data.

Sample Data

Solution Number	Concentration of FeSCN²⁺ in Solution (mol/L)	Absorbance
1	0.15	0.623
2	0.12	0.486
3	0.09	0.365
4	0.06	0.243
5	0.03	0.128
?	Unknown	0.436

Concentration of FeSCN²⁺ in the unknown solution ____0.105 mol/L____

y	ax + b
a	4.11
b	-9×10^{-4}
r	0.9995

Case Analysis Answers

1. Write the equation for the line in the form $y = ax + b$, using the values for a and b that you recorded in the Evidence Record. For example, if a = 3 and b = 6, then the equation for the line is $y = 3x + 6$.

    Answers will vary. For the sample data, $y = 4.11x - 9 \times 10^{-4}$.

2. Use the equation to calculate the concentration of FeSCN²⁺ in the unknown solution. How does the value you calculate compare with the value you read from the graph?

    Answers will vary. For the sample data, $y = 4.11x - 9 \times 10^{-4}$.

$$x = \frac{y + 9 \times 10^{-4}}{4.11} = \frac{0.436 + 9 \times 10^{-4}}{4.11} = 0.106 \text{ mol/L}$$

The equation and the graph yield almost the same value for the FeSCN²⁺ concentration.

3. The volume of the cyanide solution that was found at the scene was 20 mL. Based on the calculated concentration of $FeSCN^{2+}$ in the unknown solution, determine the concentration of potassium cyanide, KCN, in the original poison. Show all your work. Give your answer in milligrams of KCN per milliliter of solution.

(Hint: One mole of KCN will produce one mole of $FeSCN^{2+}$. Assume that all of the KCN in the poisoned solution reacted to form $FeSCN^{2+}$. Assume that the 20 mL of original solution was not diluted during the reaction to form $FeSCN^{2+}$ and that the sample you received was also undiluted. The molecular weight of $FeSCN^{2+}$ is 114 g/mol. The molecular weight of KCN is 65 g/mol.)

Answers will vary, depending on the concentration of $FeSCN^{2+}$ that you use in the unknown. A sample calculation for an unknown concentration of 0.105 mol/L is given below:

$$\frac{0.105 \text{ mmol FeSCN}^{2+}}{1 \text{ mL solution}} \times 20 \text{ mL solution} = 2.1 \text{ mmol FeSCN}^{2+} = 2.1 \text{ mmol KCN in original solution}$$

$$2.1 \text{ mmol KCN} \times 65 \text{ mg/mmol} = 137 \text{ mg KCN in original solution}$$

$$\frac{137 \text{ mg KCN}}{20 \text{ mL solution}} = 6.83 \text{ mg KCN/mL solution}$$

4. For most people, swallowing 300 mg of KCN is fatal. Based on the concentration of KCN in the poison that you calculated in question 3, determine the approximate volume of poison that the victim would have to have swallowed for it to have killed him. Show all your work.

Answers will vary depending on the concentration of KCN in the original solution. A sample calculation for a 6.83 mg/mL KCN solution is given below:

$$\frac{1 \text{ mL solution}}{6.83 \text{ mg KCN}} \times 300 \text{ mg KCN} = 44 \text{ mL solution, or about 1.49 oz}$$

5. Is it likely that the poison was the direct cause of death? Explain your answer. (Hint: Remember that the vial was mostly empty and may, at one time, have held more than 20 mL.)

In this case, it seems likely that the victim swallowed enough cyanide to kill him, given the size of the vial.

6. Suppose you found out that the concentration of $FeSCN^{2+}$ in the unknown was actually very different from the value you calculated in question 2 and the value you read off the graph. What factors could have caused that to happen?

Factors that can cause error include inaccurately prepared standards, an uncalibrated or improperly calibrated Colorimeter, equipment error, impurities in the standard or unknown solutions, and mistakes in following the procedures.

Case File 10

Dropped at the Scene: Blood spatter analysis

Analyze blood spatter evidence and help identify Jessica Barnes' killer.

Re: Police Detective Status: Barnes Murder

Museum curator Jessica Barnes was found dead on 10/05/05, the day before the grand opening of the world famous traveling exhibit Shadows of Egypt. Her body was found at the base of the large marble fountain in the center of the museum lobby.

It was clear that the victim was strangled. A few drops of blood were found on the tile floor, but blood tests show that the blood is not the victim's. Investigators have found traces of the same blood on the knuckles of the victim's hand. Investigators are suggesting that she fought her attacker, giving him or her a bloody nose or lip, and that the blood dripped onto the floor as the attacker fled the scene.

The small volume of blood suggests that the wound was minor and, thus, would have nearly healed by the time the suspects were apprehended. Indeed, none of the prime suspects showed evidence of a facial injury of any kind.

We may be able to narrow down the height of the killer from the blood spatter evidence. (We need this to order blood tests.)

Blood drops

Barnes Murder

Suspect List

Three other museum employees were working after hours the night Ms. Barnes was killed:

<u>Abraham Stein</u>, photo archivist: 6'2"/ brown eyes/ brown hair
- knew Barnes was trying to cut funding for his vintage photo department

<u>Ellie Walsh</u>, museum curator: 5'3"/ green eyes/ brown hair
- was a candidate for the head curator position six months ago, along with Barnes—Barnes given position

<u>Keith Hartman</u>, administrative assistant: 5'8"/ blue eyes/ bleached blond hair
- was recently fired by Barnes and finishing his remaining two weeks in the position

---

Forensics Objective

- determine the height of a source of blood spatters or drops

Science and Mathematics Objectives

- graph data to find quantitative relationships
- create a standard reference curve for comparison with unknown data

Materials (for each group)

- TI-83/TI-84 Plus™ Family
- newspaper
- 13 pieces of white paper
- disposable pipettes or droppers
- simulated blood
- calipers, or compass and metric ruler
- meterstick

Procedure

Part I: Collecting the Data ● ● ●

1. Create blood spatters from known heights and compare them with unknown samples.
    a) Spread newspaper on the ground. Place a piece of white paper on the newspaper.
    b) Fill a pipette with simulated blood. Drop a single drop onto the white paper from a height of 10 cm.
    c) Measure the diameter of the spatter in millimeters, using calipers or a compass. (Note: If the spatter has a ragged edge, measure *only* the diameter of the main blood drop; do *not* include any ragged edges in your measurement.) Record the diameter in the Evidence Record, along with any observations you can make about the shape of the spatter.
    d) Repeat steps 1b and 1c twice more, moving the pipette to slightly different locations but maintaining a height of 10 cm.
    e) Calculate the average diameter of the spatter that fell from 10 cm, and record it in the Evidence Record.
    f) Replace the white paper with a clean sheet. Repeat steps 1b–1e from a height of 20 cm.
    g) Repeat step 1f for each remaining height in the Evidence Record.
    h) Now measure the diameter of each spatter in the crime scene evidence, calculate the average diameter of the crime scene spatters, and enter the data into the Evidence Record.

2. Enter the height and diameter data into lists in your calculator.
    a) Press ⟨STAT⟩ ⟨ENTER⟩ to enter the data list editor.

If there are old data in any of the lists, clear them by using the arrow keys to select the list heading (L1, L2, etc.) and then pressing ⟨CLEAR⟩ ⟨ENTER⟩.

    b) In list L1, enter the heights that the drops fell.
    c) Enter the average diameter of the spatters in list L2. (Do *not* enter the data from the crime scene into the lists.)

Part II: Analyzing the Data ● ● ●

3. Start your analysis by graphing the drop height versus the average spatter diameter.
    a) Press ⟨2nd⟩ ⟨Y=⟩ to enter the Stat Plot menu.

Make sure all the other graphs are turned off before you plot your data. To turn off all other plots, select option **4: PlotsOff** before proceeding with step 3b.

b) Choose **Plot1** by pressing ⌧ENTER. On the resulting screen, turn on the plot by using the arrow keys and pressing ⌧ENTER when **On** is highlighted.

c) Choose a dot (scatter) graph, the first of the pictured graphs, by using the arrow keys and pressing ⌧ENTER when the first pictured graph is highlighted.

d) Plot the heights of the drops on the x-axis by selecting L1 (press ⌧2nd ⌧1) for the **Xlist**. Plot the diameters of the splatters on the y-axis by selecting L2 (press ⌧2nd ⌧2) for the **Ylist**. Press ⌧ENTER.

e) To set the scaling values for the graph window, press ⌧ZOOM. Select option **9: Zoom Stat** to have the calculator automatically set the window scaling to fit your data.

f) Examine the graph of your data points. Do they seem to fall along a straight line or a curve?

4. In order to figure out what kind of relationship there is between height and blood spatter diameter, you will now test several different types of curves to see which gives the best fit to your data. To determine which type of curve fits the data best, you will need to compare the r^2 values for the different fits. An r^2 value near 1 means that a curve fits the data very well. To have the calculator find r^2 values for the different curves, turn on its Diagnostic function.

a) Press ⌧2nd ⌧0 to enter the calculator's function catalog.

b) Use the arrow keys to scroll down until **DiagnosticOn** is highlighted. Press ⌧ENTER to select **DiagnosticOn**, and then press ⌧ENTER again to execute the function. **Done** will appear on your Home screen if you have done this correctly.

5. The first curve you will attempt to fit to your data will be a linear curve (a straight line). Perform a linear regression on the data to determine an equation that will allow you to predict the height a blood drop fell from if you know the size of the spatter it left behind.

a) Press ⌧STAT ⌧▷ to select the **CALC** menu.

b) Select option **4: LinReg(ax+b)**, and the LinReg program should appear on your Home screen.

c) To tell the calculator to calculate an equation relating the data in list L1 to the data in list L2, press ⌧2nd ⌧1 ⌧, ⌧2nd ⌧2 ⌧,.

d) Tell the calculator to store the data in variable Y1 by pressing ⌧VARS ⌧▷ ⌧ENTER ⌧ENTER.

e) Press ⌧ENTER to execute the linear regression. A table will print out on your screen; it will give the equation describing your data, the coefficients for the equation, and the r^2 value.

f) Record the equation and the r^2 value to four decimal places in the Evidence Record.

6. Next, try to fit a natural logarithm curve to the data. Repeat step 5 with these modifications:

a) In step 5b, select option **9: LnReg**.

b) In step 5d, tell the calculator to store the equation in variable Y2 by pressing ⌧VARS ⌧▷ ⌧ENTER, scrolling down to **Y2**, and pressing ⌧ENTER.

7. Try to fit a quadratic curve to the data. Repeat step 5 with the following modifications:

a) In step 5b, select option **5: QuadReg**.

b) In step 5d, tell the calculator to store the equation in variable Y3.

8. Try to fit a power curve to the data. Repeat step 5 with the following modifications:

a) In step 5b, select option **A: PwrReg**.

b) In step 5d, tell the calculator to store the equation in variable Y4.

9. Next, determine which type of curve best fits your data.

a) Examine the r^2 values of the four different curves recorded in your Evidence Record. The curve with the r^2 value closest to 1 best fits your data.

b) Press ⌧Y= to see the list of variables. Determine which equation best fits your data. Use the arrow keys and ⌧CLEAR to delete the equations for the other types of curves.

c) Record the equation of the best fit curve in the Evidence Record.

d) To see a graph of your data with the best fitting curve, press ⟨GRAPH⟩.

10. Estimate the height from which the blood at the crime scene fell by comparing it to your known data.

a) To trace the graph, press ⟨TRACE⟩ and then ⌃ to move from the individual data points to the graph. When the line is selected, the equation of the line will be shown at the top of the screen.

b) Use the arrow keys to trace the line until the value of the **Y =** at the bottom of the screen is as close as possible to the average diameter of the blood spatters from the crime scene.

c) Record the **X =** number from the bottom of the screen. This is the estimated height, in centimeters, from which the blood at the crime scene fell.

NAME: _____

DATE: _____

Evidence Record

Height (cm)	Diameter of Drop 1 (mm)	Diameter of Drop 2 (mm)	Diameter of Drop 3 (mm)	Average Diameter of Drops (mm)	Shape and General Observations of Blood Splatters
10					
20					
30					
40					
50					
60					
80					
100					
120					
140					
160					
180					
200					
Crime Scene					

r^2 value for linear fit (rounded to four decimal places): _____

r^2 value for natural logarithm fit: _____

r^2 value for quadratic fit: _____

r^2 value for power curve fit: _____

type of curve that gives best fit to data: _____

equation for best fit: **Y**= _____

calculated height of spatters from crime scene: **X**= _____

Case Analysis

1. Which type of curve gave the best fit to your data?
2. Did the shape of the blood spatters change as the height increased? Explain.
3. Which of the suspects could have created the blood spatters at the crime scene? Explain.
4. How accurate do you think your height estimate is? What factors can contribute to inaccuracy in your estimate? How can you reduce the errors from these factors?
5. Forensic scientists often do tests to determine the relationship between height and spatter diameter for the different cases they are involved in. What factors can cause the relationship between height and spatter diameter to differ from crime scene to crime scene?

Case File 10
Dropped at the Scene: Blood spatter analysis

Teacher Notes

Teaching time: two class periods

This lab introduces students to the science behind blood spatter analysis. It also provides a clear demonstration of the relationship between r^2 values and the goodness of fit of various curves.

Tips

- If students are having difficulty grasping the relationship between r^2 and goodness of fit, you can have them graph the various types of curves, along with their data, to show that some curves follow the data well while others don't. Simply press GRAPH after computing each type of curve to see the data with the curve superimposed. Press TRACE and then use the arrow keys to move between the different curves and the data.
- Case File 1, Tracks of a Killer, follows similar procedures. Refer students to screen shots in that activity if they are having trouble.

Lab Preparation

- Synthetic blood can be purchased from scientific supply houses, or you can use milk or Pepto-Bismol™ with a little red food coloring.
- Before class, you will need to create the crime scene evidence by dropping 3 drops of simulated blood from a known height between 10 and 200 cm. Use the "blood" and dropper type that your students will use. Select the height so that one or more of the suspects are implicated (depending on how clear-cut you want your students' results to be). Keep in mind that someone who is 5 ft tall could not create a blood drop that falls from 6 ft if the drop were produced by a nosebleed, but someone who is 6 ft tall *could* produce a drop from 5 ft if he or she bent over after being hit. The spatters you create should be given to the students as part of the evidence.
- This activity is best done in groups of at least two so that the students are able to measure heights and create spatters at the same time.
- Using dropper bottles instead of pipettes may be less messy.
- You may want to let spatters dry before measuring.

Resources

http://www.bloodspatter.com/BPATutorial.htm
Blood Stain Pattern Analysis Tutorial includes examples of origin determination and impact velocity calculation.

http://www.benecke.com/bloodspatteraafs2005.html
The short, scholarly article at this site discusses the effects of surface structure and drop height on blood spatter patterns.

Modifications

- For less-advanced students, eliminate steps 6–8 and stick with a linear fit (or choose another single curve that seems to fit your particular situation better).
- If time is short, collect fewer data on known-height blood drops.

- For more-advanced students, create crime scene evidence by dropping blood from a height outside the range of the heights the students will measure. In this case, it will be necessary for the students to use the equation for the best fit curve to calculate the approximate height of the crime scene drops. You may also allow the students to try other types of curves, such as exponential or logistic.
- If extra time is available, have students perform the experiment on different types of surfaces (e.g., carpet, cardboard, towels, wood, tile) to determine how the relationship between height and spatter size can change from one surface to another. Alternatively, give each group a different surface to experiment with and then compare the results.
- As an extension activity to introduce more mathematics, have the students determine a relationship between angle of impact and the shape of the resulting spatter. The resources given above contain additional information on how to do it.

Sample Data (using Pepto-Bismol)

Height (cm)	Diameter of Drop 1 (mm)	Diameter of Drop 2 (mm)	Diameter of Drop 3 (mm)	Average Diameter of Drops (mm)	Shape and General Observations of Blood Splatters
10	7	7	7	7	
20	10	10	12	10.7	
30	10	13	12	11.7	
40	14	12	13	13	
50	12	13	13	12.7	
60	14	14	14	14	
80	15	16	15	15.3	
100	17	17	17	17	
120	18	18	18	18	
140	18	18	18	18	
160	18	18	18	18	
180	20	20	20	20	
200	20	20	20	20	
Crime Scene	11	12	11	11.3	

r^2 value for linear fit (rounded to four decimal places): _____0.8909_____

r^2 value for natural logarithm fit: _____0.978_____

r^2 value for quadratic fit: _____0.9582_____

r^2 value for power curve fit: ___0.9679_____

type of curve that gives best fit to data: ___natural logarithm_____

equation for best fit: **Y**= ___⁻2.77 + 4.23 lnX_____

calculated height of spatters from crime scene: **X**= _____27.4 cm_____

(equation for linear fit: **Y1 = .058X + 9.7**)

(equation for quadratic fit: **Y3 = -3.22E $^-$ 4X^2+0.124X+7.57**)

(equation for power curve fit: **Y4 = 3.75X$^{0.123}$**)

Case Analysis Answers

1. Which type of curve gave the best fit to your data?
   Answers may vary. In this case, the natural logarithm gave the best fit to the data. However, the relationship between height and diameter can vary, depending on the nature of the surface and the "blood" used.
2. Did the shape of the blood spatters change as the height increased? Explain.
   Answers may vary. Drops that fall greater distances may have more ragged edges because they are moving more quickly when they hit. Drops that fall farther may also form secondary drops as liquid bounces off the paper.
3. Which of the suspects could have created the blood spatters at the crime scene? Explain.
   In this case, any of the three suspects could have produced the spatters because the approximate height is only about 30 cm. Students should indicate the understanding that blood drops of a certain height can be produced by someone taller than that height but are not likely to be produced by someone shorter than that height.
4. How accurate do you think your height estimate is? What factors can contribute to inaccuracy in your estimate? How can you reduce the errors from these factors?
   Answers may vary. Inaccuracies in drop height estimates can arise from a variety of sources, including inaccurate or imprecise measurement of test drops and heights, relatively poor fit of the bestfit curve, too few data points collected, and differences between the experimental and actual conditions (e.g., surfaces, air temperature and humidity, wind conditions).
5. Forensic scientists often do tests to determine the relationship between height and spatter diameter for the different cases they are involved in. What factors can cause the relationship between height and spatter diameter to differ from crime scene to crime scene?
   Factors that can influence the shape and/or size of a blood splatter include the following: consistency of the blood (although it is generally stable, it can change within a certain range); speed at which the drops are traveling; angle at which the drops hit the surface; type of surface the drops are hitting; amount of time between when the spatters were made and when they were measured; and environmental conditions at the scene (e.g., temperature, wind, humidity).

Case File 11

Ashes to Ashes: Using evaporation rate to identify an unknown liquid

Measure and compare the cooling rates of unknown liquids, and identify the probable arsonist.

<u>**PROBABLE ARSON**</u>

Investigator: James

Date: 10/05/05

- call in at 3:04 a.m.
- large fire on the East Side; historic log cabin of town founder, James McDonald
- first responders too late to save cabin
- traces of an unidentified chemical residue discovered in cabin remains
- drops of unidentified chemical found between cabin remains and main road

   (??accelerant used to spread the fire??)

   <u>ARSON strongly suspected</u>
- chemical evidence sent to lab for testing

McDonald Cabin Arson
Suspect List
  The following four people were found within three blocks of the blaze
  in the early morning and were brought in for questioning. Each has
  access to flame accelerants for one reason or another. Chemicals
  collected from each of the suspects have been sent to the lab for
  identification and comparison with those collected at the scene.

Suspect 1: Barney Weber: member of school custodial staff
Weber was found cleaning out the back of his truck several blocks from
the crime scene.
Suspect 2: Anna Appleby: local painter and muralist
Police found Appleby finishing a mural on a warehouse wall across the
street from the fire.
Suspect 3: Virginia Lawson Smith: mechanic
Lawson Smith called the fire department. Police questioning her found
chemicals on her work clothes.
Suspect 4: Dr. Martin Brown: university chemist
Brown was transporting a cart of chemicals to his college laboratory
when police picked him up.

Forensics Objective

- identify the likely accelerant in an arson

Science and Mathematics Objectives

- identify a solution, based on evaporation rate
- understand that evaporation rate is a characteristic property of a liquid

Materials (for each group)

- TI-83/TI-84 Plus™ Family
- Vernier EasyTemp™ temperature probe
- Vernier EasyData™ application
- accelerant samples from 4 suspects
- accelerant sample from crime scene
- 5 small test tubes
- test-tube rack
- 6 pieces of filter paper cut into 2 × 2 cm squares
- 6 small rubber bands
- lint-free tissues or paper towels
- goggles (1 pair per student)

Procedure

In order to determine whether any of the accelerants found with the suspects matched the accelerant found at the crime scene, you will need to compare the evaporation rate of each suspect's sample with the evaporation rate of the sample from the crime scene. You will compare the samples by, first, graphing the temperature change of each sample as it evaporates and, second, comparing the graphs of each sample to look for a match. Because your calculator can display only three curves at a time on a graph, you will need to create two different graphs with three curves (two suspect samples and the crime scene sample) on each graph.

1. Connect the EasyTemp temperature probe to the USB port on your calculator.

2. To set up the EasyData App for data collection, select ⌈File⌉ from the Main screen, and then select ⌈New⌉ to reset the application. The Main screen should be displayed. You should see the current temperature reading at the top of the screen and **Mode: Time Graph: 180 (s)** near the bottom of the screen.

> At the bottom of the Main screen are five options (⌈File⌉, ⌈Setup⌉, ⌈Start⌉, ⌈Graph⌉, and ⌈Quit⌉). Each of these options can be selected by pressing the calculator key located below it (〈Y=〉, 〈WINDOW〉, 〈ZOOM〉, 〈TRACE〉, or 〈GRAPH〉).

3. The default experimental setup is to collect one sample every second for 180 seconds. For this experiment, you will need to collect one sample every second for 240 seconds. Change the length of the experiment to 240 seconds.
   a) Select ⌈Setup⌉ from the Main screen.
   b) Select **2: Time Graph**.
   c) Select ⌈Edit⌉ to change the values. The default sample interval is 1 second, which is what we want for this experiment. Select [Next] to move to the next option.
   d) Press 〈CLEAR〉 to remove the default number of samples (180), and type **240** as the number of samples.
   e) Select ⌈Next⌉.

---

f) Confirm that the settings are correct (sample interval = 1 second, number of samples = 240, experiment length = 240 seconds) and then select 〔OK〕.

Obtain and wear goggles! CAUTION: The compounds used in this experiment are flammable and poisonous. Avoid inhaling their vapors. Avoid touching them with your skin or clothing. Be sure there are no open flames, heat sources, or sparks in the lab during this experiment. Notify your teacher immediately if an accident occurs.

4. Wrap the probe with a square of filter paper, and secure the paper with a small rubber band, as shown in the figure.

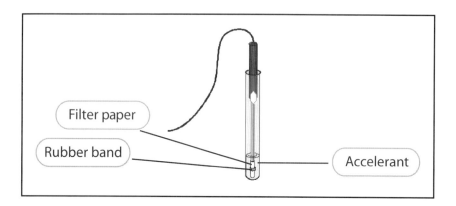

5. Pour a small amount of the accelerant from Suspect 1 into a test tube. Place the test tube in a test-tube rack, and place the temperature probe into the test tube so that the filter paper is covered by the liquid.

6. After the probe has been in the liquid for at least 30 seconds, select 〔Start〕 to begin collecting temperature data. On the calculator screen, a real-time graph of temperature vs. time will be displayed. The temperature readings are displayed in the upper right corner of the graph.
   a) Leave the temperature probe in the test tube for 15 seconds to establish the initial temperature of the liquid.
   b) Remove the probe from the liquid, and tape it to the table so the tip of the probe extends over the edge of the tabletop.

7. Data collection will stop after 240 seconds. The graph of temperature vs. time will then be scaled and displayed. The time, **X**, and temperature, **Y**, values are displayed above the graph.
   a) Use the arrow keys to move along the graph and determine the maximum and minimum temperatures for this sample. Record the maximum temperature as the T_{max} in your Evidence Record, and record the minimum temperature as T_{min}.
   b) Subtract the minimum temperature from the maximum temperature to determine the temperature change during evaporation. Record this value in the Evidence Record.

8. To store the data that you collected during this run, select 〔Main〕 to return to the Main screen. Select 〔File〕 and choose option **5: Store Run...**. If you get a message about overwriting stored data, select 〔OK〕.

9. Remove the rubber band, dispose of the filter, and dry the probe thoroughly.

10. Repeat steps 4–9 with the accelerant from Suspect 2.

11. With the accelerant from the crime scene, repeat steps 4–7 *only*. (*Careful! Do not* store this run, or your data will be overwritten.)

12. Plot the data from all three accelerants on the same graph.
   a) Select ⌈Adv⌉.
   b) Select **7↓L2, L3 and L4 vs L1**.

13. Compare the graphs to decide whether either Suspect 1 or Suspect 2 had an accelerant that is likely to be the same as the accelerant used at the crime scene.
   a) If one of the suspects' accelerants produces a plot that matches the shape of the plot from the crime scene accelerant, it could be the accelerant that was used.
   b) To identify which plot corresponds to which accelerant, use ⊙ and ⊙ to move the cursor from plot to plot and match the T_{max} and T_{min} values to those in your Evidence Record. See the example.

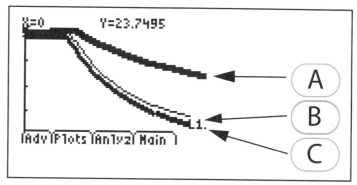

You can see that curves B and C are nearly identical in shape. Curve B is from the crime scene. Accelerant C is most likely to have been the accelerant used at the crime scene.

14. Even if you got a match in step 13, you need to test and compare the other two accelerants; two of the accelerants could be the same. Select ⌈Main⌉ to return to the Main screen. Repeat steps 4–13 for the accelerants from Suspect 3 and Suspect 4 and the accelerant from the crime scene. (Remember, *do not* perform a **Store As** for the crime scene run.)

NAME: _____

DATE: _____

Evidence Record

Substance	T_{max} (°C)	T_{min} (°C)	$T_{max} - T_{min}$ (°C)	Cooling-Rate Graph Match?
Suspect 1				
Suspect 2				
Suspect 3				
Suspect 4				
Crime Scene				NA

Case Analysis

1. Which of the suspects' accelerants best matches the accelerant from the crime scene?
2. Did any of the suspects' accelerants appear to be the same liquid? If so, which ones?
3. Why may the graphs of the crime scene accelerant and primary suspect's accelerant not match exactly?
4. In what other ways can you examine the accelerants to determine which one was used in the crime?

Case File 11
Ashes to Ashes: Using evaporation rate to identify an unknown liquid

Teacher Notes

Teaching time: one to two class periods

This lab introduces the concept of evaporation rate and teaches students how to plot more than one curve on a graph.

Tips

Have students work in groups. You may want to use a different "crime scene accelerant" for each group.

Lab Preparation

Materials (accelerants) per group
- 10 mL methanol
- 10 mL acetone
- 10 mL isopropanol
- 10 mL *tert*-butyl alcohol

Setup notes
- The filter paper is necessary to slow down the evaporation process.
- Small rubber bands used for braces work very well. Small hair ties are another possibility.
- Put out the smallest test tubes you have. There is no reason for each group to have much of these solutions.
- Label test tubes with suspect numbers or names from the investigation report.

Background Information

In this lab, students use the evaporation rate as a characteristic property with which to distinguish different liquids from one another. The evaporation rate of a liquid depends primarily upon the volatility of the liquid, the temperature of the surrounding air, and the air pressure. Temperature change is a good proxy for evaporation rate because the evaporation of each liquid causes a decrease in its temperature; the faster the liquid evaporates, the faster the temperature drops.

In real arson investigations, gas chromatography, rather than tests of evaporation rates, is usually used to identify accelerants. This is necessary for several reasons: 1) many accelerants are nonvolatile or solid substances; 2) it is rare to find unadulterated accelerant samples near the site of an arson; and 3) trace impurities are often present in different accelerants. Identifying and matching these impurities to other samples can help investigators tie a suspect or a particular batch of accelerant to a particular fire. Many of these impurities do not significantly change evaporation rate, so they could not be detected by the method used in this lab.

Differences in evaporation rate can be difficult to measure and are not as accurate in establishing the identity of an accelerant as is gas chromatography. However, many of the factors that affect evaporation rate also produce distinctive patterns in gas chromatograms. Gas chromatography, like other forms of chromatography, separates the components of a mixture according to their affinities for a particular substrate. These affinities are often related to the same molecular characteristics that cause a substance to be highly volatile or relatively stable. For example, a substance with highly polar bonds will probably have a low evaporation rate; the polar bonds will probably also affect its relationship to the gas chromatography substrate. Therefore, even though the students are not necessarily using the same *method* to identify accelerants in this lab, the method they are using is based upon the same chemical principles.

Resources

http://www.firearson.com/
This Web site for the International Association of Arson Investigators contains many links and a great deal of interesting information.

Modifications

- It may be difficult to complete this lab in one period. If time is an issue, have students investigate only two of the suspects (delete step 14).
- If a computer with TI Connect™ software is available, the accelerant samples can be compared all at the same time using the following set of procedures. This set of procedures requires a working knowledge of opening files and making graphs in Microsoft Excel®. If you or your students are unfamiliar with making graphs, refer to the Help menu in Excel.
- If you choose to use the computer to display the data, use the following steps after step 6:

7. Data collection will stop after 240 seconds. The graph of temperature vs. time will then be scaled and displayed.

8. Remove the rubber band, dispose of the filter, and dry the probe thoroughly.

9. To store the data you collected during this run, select 〔**Main**〕 to return to the Main screen. Select 〔**File**〕 and choose option **5: Store Run....** If you get a message about overwriting stored data, select 〔**OK**〕.

10. In order to compare many different accelerants at the same time, you will transfer your temperature data from your calculator to a computer, using TI Connect. Transfer the temperature data from the first run.
    a) From the Main screen, select 〔**Quit**〕 then 〔**OK**〕. This will return you to the Home screen.
    b) Disconnect the temperature probe from the calculator.
    c) Connect the calculator to the computer with the USB cable by plugging the cable into the USB port on the computer *before* plugging the other end into the calculator.
    d) Start TI Connect by double-clicking the desktop icon.
    e) Once you have opened TI Connect, select TI DeviceExplorer. (Note: Make sure your calculator is turned on *before* selecting TI DeviceExplorer.)
    f) The DeviceExplorer screen will display a list of the different files in your calculator. Double-click on List (Real) to open the data lists. (Note: It may take a few seconds for the computer to talk to your calculator. Be patient!)
    g) You will need to transfer the data in the lists to the TI DataEditor. On the DeviceExplorer menu bar, select Tools and then TI DataEditor.
    h) The time data for the first run are stored in list L1. Click and drag "L1" from the DeviceEx-plorer to the DataEditor. (Note: You may need to move the windows around on your computer screen until you can see both the DeviceExplorer and the DataEditor windows.)
    i) When the time data have finished transferring, transfer the temperature data for the first run (stored in list L2) by clicking and dragging "L2" from the DeviceExplorer to the DataEditor.
    j) Right-click on the L1 column label in the DataEditor and select Properties. Under Variable Name, click the radio button at the very bottom and type "TIME" in the box.
    k) Repeat step 10j for the L2 column, but type the name "TEMP1."
    l) From the DataEditor menu bar, select File, then select Special List Export. Type a name for your data file and click Save. (Note: Be sure to select Special List Export, not just Export; Export will save *only* the first column of your data!)
    m) Disconnect the USB cable from your calculator. Leave the cable connected to your computer for the next run.
    n) Reconnect the EasyTemp probe to the USB port on your calculator. The EasyData screen should come up and display the ambient temperature. You are now ready to collect data for the next accelerant.

11. Repeat steps 4–10 with the remaining accelerants, but make the following changes:
    a) Skip step 10j.
    b) In step 10k, type the name "TEMPX" for the L2 column, where X is the number representing which sample the data are from (TEMP1 for Suspect 1, TEMP2 for Suspect 2, TEMP3 for Suspect 3, TEMP4 for Suspect 4, and TEMP5 for the crime scene).
    c) Do not type a new name for the file in the next step (10l). Use the same name you used before. When the computer asks if you want to overwrite the file, click Yes.

12. Use Microsoft Excel to compare the cooling graphs of the data.
    a) Open Excel. From the menu bar, choose File > Open. Open the file containing your temperature data. (Note: In order to see the file that you created, you may need to select Files of Type: All files (*.*). The DataEditor saves the data as a .csv file.)
    b) Using Excel, create a line graph of the cooling curves for each accelerant. Plot time on the x-axis and temperature on the y-axis. Compare the curves of the four accelerants to the curve of the accelerant from the crime scene.
    c) Decide which suspect is most likely to be guilty.

Sample Data

(Note: This Evidence Record is not necessary if the students use TI Connect™ software and Microsoft Excel™ to analyze their data.)

Substance	T_{max} (°C)	T_{min} (°C)	$T_{max} - T_{min}$ (°C)	Cooling-Rate Graph Match?
Suspect 1 (Methanol)	25.4	8.1	17.3	No
Suspect 2 (Acetone)	22.6	6.3	16.3	Yes
Suspect 3 (Isopropanol)	23.8	16.8	7	No
Suspect 4 (*tert*-Butyl Alcohol)	24.6	19.9	4.7	No
Crime Scene (Acetone)	23.7	9.6	14.1	NA

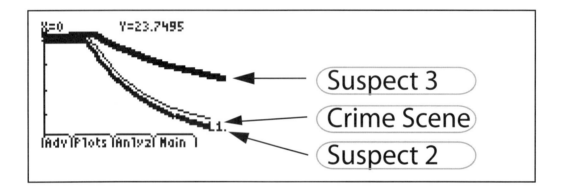

Guilty suspect: Suspect 2

Case Analysis Answers

1. Which of the suspects' accelerants best matches the accelerant from the crime scene?
   Answers will vary.
2. Did any of the suspects' accelerants appear to be the same liquid? If so, which ones?
   Answers will vary.
3. Why may the graphs of the crime scene accelerant and primary suspect's accelerant not match exactly?
   There may be differences in the amount of liquid on the probe, impurities in one or both of the samples, variations in ambient temperature or humidity, or differences in the starting temperature of the samples.
4. In what other ways can you examine the accelerants to determine which one was used in the crime?
   Answers may vary. (Boiling point is probably the most useful.)

Case File 12

Hit and Run:
Using information from an event data recorder to reconstruct an accident

Replicate data from an event data recorder to identify the culprit in a hit and run.

Police Report

Rania Sallum, 58, was struck by a large, dark-colored SUV Wednesday around 7:20 a.m. Sallum could not see the driver or read the license plate, but she knows that she was struck by the front right bumper of the vehicle, which then slowed almost to a stop before speeding off. She estimates that the incident occurred between 7:15 and 7:25 a.m. A hit-and-run bulletin and vehicle description went out to all officers. Three police teams spotted vehicles with front right bumper damage and recorded the following information from their drivers:

Natalya Ludnova, 25--pulled over for speeding when the officer noticed bumper damage—claimed that damage was due to hitting the curb while parking.

Everett Smalls, 38--brought in for blocking a fire lane—claimed that bumper was damaged in a stop-and-go rush hour fender bender.

Antonia Angeles, 53--pulled over for speeding when the officer noticed bumper damage—claimed a neighbor backed into her car as she drove past his driveway.

EDR data downloaded from each car for the 10 seconds before and after the bumper collision show that each occurred between 7 and 8 a.m. Wednesday. See below.

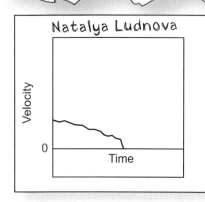

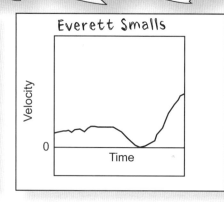

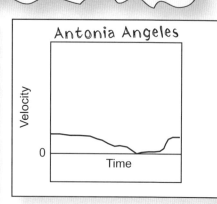

Forensics Objectives

- simulate the use of an event data recorder (EDR) in order to show how the evidence gathered by this device can be used for legal purposes
- show how accident scenes can be recreated through an analysis of the data that are gathered by an EDR

Science and Mathematics Objectives

- learn how distance traveled, velocity, and acceleration are related to one another
- learn how the appearance of an acceleration, velocity, or distance vs. time graph can be used to predict the appearance of the other graphs

Materials

- TI-83/TI-84 Plus™ Family
- Vernier EasyData™ application
- Calculator-Based Ranger 2™ (CBR 2™)
- toy car, at least 5 cm tall

Procedure

1. Connect the CBR 2 to the calculator with the USB cable. EasyData will open immediately, and the CBR 2 will begin collecting distance data. You will know when the CBR 2 is collecting data because it will be clicking.

2. Place the CBR 2 and car on a lab table or the floor. The CBR 2 should be facing the car, and they should be about 30 cm apart. Remove any surrounding objects so that the data you acquire will be relatively "noise" free.

3. Observe the calculator display to make sure that the CBR 2 is picking up the position of the car. It should show a distance of about 0.3 m.

> If the distance is not being measured in meters, select 〔Setup〕 and select option **1: Distance**. Under **Units**, choose option **1: (m)**. Exit to the Main screen by selecting 〔OK〕.

4. Perform a test run with your car. Have one team member push the car and release it. Have another team member check the readings on the calculator screen. You do not need to record the motion at this point. Just be sure that the CBR 2 is measuring the increasing distance to the car as it moves away. Also be sure that the car is pushed gently enough that it stops before the end of the table.

5. Now you are set to begin the experiment. Change the experiment parameters to have the calculator record one sample every 0.05 seconds for 3 seconds.
   a) From the Main screen, select 〔Setup〕 and choose option **2: Time Graph**.
   b) Select 〔Edit〕. To change the time between samples to 0.05 seconds, press 〔CLEAR〕 and then enter **0.05**.
   c) Select 〔Next〕 to change the number of samples that the calculator will record. Press 〔CLEAR〕 and then enter **60** for the number of samples.
   d) Select 〔Next〕 to confirm that your settings are correct. The sample interval should be 0.05 seconds; the number of samples should be 60; and the experiment length should be 3 seconds.
   e) When you have confirmed that the experiment setup is correct, select 〔OK〕 to return to the Main screen.

6. Position the team members so that one can start the EasyData App and the other can push the car away from the CBR 2.

7. Select [Start] to begin collecting data. (You may also have to select [OK] to overwrite the last run.) As soon as data collection begins, push the car away from the CBR 2 the same way that you did in your test run. Data collection will continue for 3 seconds, and then the screen will read **Transferring Data**.

8. After the data are transferred to the calculator, a distance vs. time graph will automatically plot on the screen. Select [Plots] to examine the velocity vs. time graph as well. These graphs should be relatively smooth, indicating that you picked up the motion of the vehicle and not a lot of extraneous noise. See the sample graphs below.

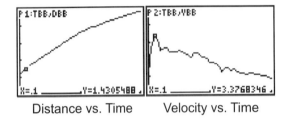

Distance vs. Time   Velocity vs. Time

If the graphs of the distance and velocity are not relatively smooth (an absolutely smooth graph is rarely observed), repeat steps 7 and 8.

9. Sketch these plots in the Evidence Record. Then complete the Case Analysis.

NAME: _____

DATE: _____

Evidence Record

Distance vs. Time

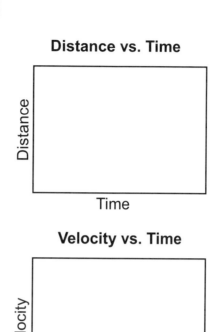

Velocity vs. Time

Case Analysis

1. Look at the velocity vs. time graph plotted by your calculator. At what time did the car begin to move?
2. What was the maximum velocity of the car?
3. At what time did the car reach its maximum velocity?
4. Look at the distance vs. time graph plotted by your calculator. Does the time at which the car's distance from the CBR 2 increased match the time in question 1?
5. How far did the car move before it reached its maximum velocity?

Use the arrow keys to move the cursor along the graph. To change the type of plot that is displayed without changing the position of the cursor, select [Plots] and then select the graph you want to see.

6. EDRs in vehicles record information on velocity and acceleration for moving vehicles. The data recorded by EDRs help reconstruct the events of an accident. For example, data from the EDR can show when a car's brakes were applied, if at all.

   Suppose a vehicle were traveling at a constant speed, using cruise control, when suddenly the brakes were applied until the vehicle stopped. Sketch a velocity vs. time graph for this situation. Label the point at which the brakes were applied and the point at which the vehicle came to a complete stop.

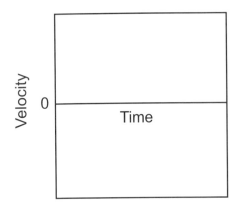

7. Do the EDR data taken from the suspects support their stories? Do the EDR graphs suggest that any of these suspects is the culprit in the hit and run? Explain your answers.

Case File 12
Hit and Run:
Using information from an event data recorder to reconstruct an accident

Teacher Notes

Teaching time: one class period

This lab introduces students to the concept that displacement, velocity, and acceleration are related quantities and that patterns in one can be used to predict patterns in the others.

Tips

*   Position the CBR 2 behind the toy car. Select (Start), wait an instant, and then push the car. Be sure that the CBR 2 records the push and release. These are important points on the velocity and acceleration graphs.
*   Be sure that the students have chosen option **2: Time Graph** under the (Setup) menu (Procedure step 5a). Otherwise, the data for distance and velocity will not be saved.

Lab Preparation

*   The are only a few things necessary for this lab: a toy car large enough to be picked up by the CBR 2, a CBR 2 attached to a calculator with the EasyData App, and a clear space on the floor or a long table to roll the car on.
*   A toy car or truck at least 5 cm high works well with the CBR 2.

Background Information

Event data recorders, or automobile black boxes, can make many contributions to automobile safety; however, they also raise many important questions concerning an individual's right to privacy. The balance of these two seemingly conflicting objectives is one of the dilemmas of life in the technological age.

The relationship between the two graphs (distance vs. time and velocity vs. time) that the CBR 2 generates is important for students to understand. They should learn the fundamentals of how the behavior of one graph can predict the appearance of the other graph. For example, when the velocity is positive and increasing, the vehicle is moving away from the CBR 2.

Modifications

*   If your students are more advanced, you can have them examine the acceleration vs. time graphs available on the calculator at Procedure step 8. You can also have them sketch or predict the shape of an acceleration vs. time graph in Case Analysis question 7. Be aware that these graphs tend to be very noisy and can be confusing unless the student is fairly comfortable with the concept of acceleration.
*   If you have access to a computer with TI Connect™, you can have students print out their graphs. TI Screen Capture will allow screen shots to be saved as .bmp, .tif, or .jpg files, which can be printed from any compatible program (e.g., Word or Paint from Microsoft®). Start Connect and attach the USB cable to the computer. Then have the students follow the directions below after they complete Procedure step 8:

    9.   Select (Plots) and select option **1: Dist(m) vs Time** to display the distance vs. time graph.

10. Disconnect the CBR 2 from the calculator. Use the USB cable that is connected to the computer to connect the calculator to the computer.
11. From the Connect main screen, select Screen Capture. Wait a few seconds for the computer to detect the calculator and load the image on the screen.
12. When an image of the graph on your calculator shows up on the Screen Capture screen, select File > Save As… to save the image to the computer's hard drive.
13. On the calculator screen, select (Plots) and then select option **2: Vel(m/s) vs Time** to display the velocity vs. time graph.
14. Repeat step 12 for the velocity vs. time graph. Both graphs can now be printed from any program that allows you to print image files.
15. When both graphs have been saved, disconnect the calculator from the computer's USB cable. Use the distance vs. time and velocity vs. time graphs to answer the Case Analysis questions.

Sample Data (using a high plastic truck with extra weight in the truck bed)

Distance vs. Time

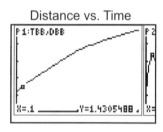

Velocity vs. Time

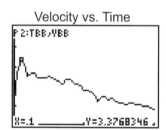

Case Analysis Answers (using results from pushing a Hall's carriage)

Distance vs. Time

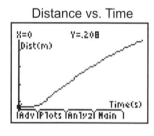

Velocity vs. Time

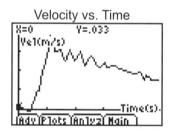

1. Look at the velocity vs. time graph plotted by your calculator. At what time did the car begin to move?
   0.3 seconds
2. What was the maximum velocity of the car?
   0.714 m/s
3. At what time did the car reach its maximum velocity?
   0.7 seconds
4. Look at the distance vs. time graph plotted by your calculator. Does the time at which the car's distance from the CBR 2 increased match the time in question 1?
   Yes
5. How far did the car move before it reached its maximum velocity?
   0.127 m
6. Suppose a vehicle were traveling at a constant speed, using cruise control, when suddenly the brakes were applied until the vehicle stopped. Sketch a velocity vs. time graph for this situation. Label the point at which the brakes were applied and the point at which the vehicle came to a complete stop.
   (Note: The details of the graph are not extremely important. The important point that the students should demonstrate is that velocity is constant (non-0) until the brakes are applied, at which time it decreases sharply before ending at constant 0.)

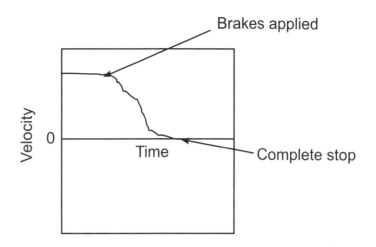

7. Do the EDR data taken from the suspects support their stories? Do the EDR graphs suggest that any of these suspects is the culprit in the hit and run? Explain your answers.

Natalya Ludnova's graph supports her story. The graph shows a sudden stop followed by no movement, which is consistent with a sudden stop while parking. The graph for Antonia Angeles supports her story; it shows a slowing and then an increase to the previous speed, which can happen with a small jolt from the side. The graphs suggest that Everett Smalls was involved in the hit and run. His EDR data show a rapid deceleration followed by a rapid acceleration. If he had been involved in a fender bender in rush hour traffic as he claimed, the EDR probably would have shown no deceleration or acceleration, or a very small amount. He almost certainly would not have been able to accelerate rapidly in rush hour traffic. Instead, it seems likely that he sped away from the hit-and-run scene.

Case File 13

Life in the Fast Lane: Using skid marks to determine vehicle speed

Estimate the speed of a vehicle from the length of its skid marks.

Car Chase Dead Ends

Police left empty handed as thieves escape on pier

HARBERTVILLE, Friday: Downtown was thrown into chaos last night as a dramatic police chase snarled traffic and sent pedestrians diving for cover. The chase was a result of a robbery at the First United Bank on Maple Blvd. Three burglars robbed the bank and escaped in an unmarked black luxury sedan.

The pursuing officers could not determine the exact make and model of the car or read the dealer's license plate taped to the back window. The police lost sight of the vehicle after the thieves reached the waterfront, skidded to a stop near the end of the pier, and turned into the adjacent loading docks.

The only evidence left at the scene was the car's skid marks. Police have located three cars that match the general description of the getaway car and that were purchased recently from Luxury Motors, the city's only luxury car dealer. Police are now working to narrow the list of suspects.

```
TO: Chief Detective
FROM: Crime Scene Investigatory Team
```

Please examine the attached photo of vehicle skid marks, recorded as 738 ft. We estimate that the vehicle was moving at top speed before skidding.

The following persons recently purchased similar sedans that fit the description of the getaway car. Their top speeds are noted.

D. J. Bitterman: Barrington Twister, top speed 105 mph
Latoya Sikes: SMC Shade, top speed 115 mph
Anwar Al-Dosari: Turner Black Bolt, top speed 140 mph

Forensics Objective

- determine the speed of a vehicle before its brakes were applied

Science and Mathematics Objectives

- determine the coefficient of friction between a vehicle and a road surface
- convert between SI units and Imperial units
- rearrange equations to solve for different variables

Materials (for each group)

- TI-83/TI-84 Plus™ Family
- Vernier EasyData™ application
- Vernier EasyLink™
- Dual-Range Force Sensor
- Hall's carriage or heavy toy car
- thread, string, or yarn
- rubber bands (for a Hall's carriage) or tissue (for a toy car)
- meterstick or metric tape measure
- C-clamp or duct tape
- chalk or tape
- flat, smooth surface (floor or table)

Procedure

Part I: Determining the Coefficient of Friction ● ● ●

1. In order to model a vehicle that is skidding, not rolling, you need to prevent its wheels from rotating. If you are using a Hall's carriage, use a tight rubber band between the axles. If you are using a toy car, stuff tissue in the wheel wells. Make sure that the vehicle slides, without the wheels moving, when you push it along.

2. Tie a 15 cm piece of thread, string, or yarn to the front end of the vehicle.

3. Connect the Dual-Range Force Sensor to EasyLink. Set the switch on the force sensor to ±10 N. Plug EasyLink into the USB port of the calculator. The calculator will turn itself on, and the EasyData screen will appear.

4. Zero the force sensor with nothing attached to it.
   a) Place the force sensor on a flat, smooth surface, with its hook parallel to the surface.
   b) Select ⎾Setup⏋ and choose option **7: Zero...**.
   c) When the force reading is fairly constant, select ⎾Zero⏋.
   d) Carefully attach the hook on the sensor to the thread connected to the vehicle. Make sure that there is no tension on the thread. The force reading on the Main screen should be 0 ± 0.01.

5. Set up the EasyData App to collect one sample every 0.02 seconds for 2 seconds.
   a) From the Main screen, select ⎾Setup⏋.
   b) Select option **2: Time Graph**.
   c) Select ⎾Edit⏋ to edit the experiment parameters.
   d) Press ⟨CLEAR⟩ and then enter **0.02** as the sample interval. Select ⎾Next⏋ to set the number of samples.
   e) Press ⟨CLEAR⟩ and then enter **100** as the number of samples. Select ⎾Next⏋.

f) When you have confirmed that the experimental parameters are correct (0.02-second sample interval, 100 samples, 2-second experiment length), select ⌐OK⌐ to return to the Main screen.

6. When you are collecting data, it is best to have one person pulling the vehicle and a second person pushing the buttons on the calculator.
   a) Using a steady force, pull on the force sensor to move the vehicle across a smooth, flat surface at as constant a speed as possible.
   b) *After* the vehicle has started moving, select ⌐Start⌐ to begin collecting data. If you get a message about overwriting data, select ⌐OK⌐.
   c) Continue pulling the vehicle at a constant speed until the calculator screen reads **Transferring Data**. (Note: Make sure the force sensor remains flat on the surface at all times. If the force sensor is lifted off the surface, your force readings will be inaccurate.)

7. Your graph will look something like the one below.

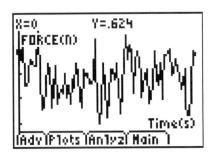

The force will look very uneven because the range on the *y*-axis is very small. As long as you pull with a constant force, your results should be fine. If your graph has any spikes or dips that are much larger than the rest, select ⌐Main⌐ to return to the Main screen and repeat steps 5 and 6.

8. Compute the average force with which you pulled the vehicle. Since the vehicle was moving at a constant speed (there was no acceleration), the force with which you pulled it was equal to the force exerted by friction (the forces were balanced).
   a) Select ⌐Anlyz⌐, then choose option **1: Statistics...**. The calculator will ask you to set the bounds for the analysis (the region of the graph that should be included in the calculations). You will be using all of the data you collected.
   b) The cursor will be at the far left side of the graph. Select ⌐OK⌐ to set this point as the left boundary.
   c) The cursor will now be at the far right side of the graph. Select ⌐OK⌐ to set this point as the right boundary.
   d) The calculator will take a second or two to calculate the mean and standard deviation. When the statistics screen appears, record the **mean** value in your Evidence Record. This is the average force with which you pulled the vehicle. Select ⌐OK⌐ then ⌐Main⌐ to return to the Main screen.

9. Weigh the vehicle.
   a) Disconnect the string from both the vehicle and the force sensor. Hold the force sensor vertically at least 30 cm above your surface so that the vehicle will not touch it when suspended from the string. Attach the string to the hook on the force sensor but not to the car.
   b) Select ⌐Setup⌐ and then select option **7: Zero...**.
   c) When the force reading is fairly constant, select ⌐Zero⌐.
   d) Carefully attach the vehicle to the thread connected to the sensor. Try not to let the vehicle swing or twist on the thread.

e) When the vehicle is hanging from the force sensor and is relatively stationary, select (Start) to collect data on the weight of the car. If you get a message about overwriting data, select (OK).

f) Let the vehicle hang from the sensor until the screen reads **Transferring Data**. Then carefully remove the vehicle from the hook on the force sensor.

g) Your screen will display a graph of force vs. time.

10. Repeat step 8, this time with the weight data, to have the calculator find the mean value, which is the average weight of the vehicle. Record this in the Evidence Record.

11. Divide the average force by which you pulled the vehicle, which equals the friction force, by the average weight of the vehicle. The result is μ, the coefficient of friction for the vehicle and the surface it skidded on. (Note: The force and weight are given in newtons, but the resulting coefficient of friction has no units because you divide newtons by newtons.) Record the coefficient of friction in your Evidence Record.

Part II: Finding Speed from Skidding Distance ● ● ●

12. Use chalk or tape to make a starting line for your measurements on the flat, smooth surface you are using.

13. Simulate the car chase by pushing the vehicle and letting it skid to a stop.
    a) Remove the string from the vehicle. Leave the vehicle's wheels locked.
    b) Place the vehicle a short distance behind the starting line, and push it toward the starting line with a constant force.
    c) Release the vehicle just as its front wheels cross the starting line.
    d) Wait until the vehicle is still, and mark the location of its front wheels.
    e) Measure the distance from the starting line to the place where the vehicle's front wheels stopped, in centimeters. Record this as the skidding distance in your Evidence Record.

14. Use the speed equation to calculate the speed that the vehicle was traveling when it crossed the starting line and began to skid. The speed equation is $v = \sqrt{2g\mu d}$ where v is velocity (speed) at the start of the skid, g is acceleration due to gravity (9.8 m/s^2), μ is the coefficient of friction, and d is the distance (in *meters*) the vehicle skidded before stopping. (Note: Be sure that the units of your measurements are consistent with one another!)

15. Repeat steps 13 and 14 at least two more times to fill in your Evidence Record.

Name: _____

Date: _____

Evidence Record

	Value
Average Sliding Friction (N) **(Equal to average force used to pull vehicle)**	
Average weight of vehicle (N)	
Coefficient of friction, μ $\mu = \dfrac{\textit{Sliding friction (N)}}{\textit{Weight of vehicle (N)}}$	

Trial Number	Skidding Distance (cm)	Speed (cm/s)
1		
2		
3		

Case Analysis

1. Rearrange the speed equation to solve for d, the skidding distance. Show your work.
2. In most cases, an accident investigator cannot accurately compute μ, the coefficient of friction. However, tests have been done to establish a range of values for μ that apply to most situations. In general, the coefficient of friction for a car on an asphalt road is between 0.5 and 0.9. Using this information and the equation from question 1, fill in the final two columns in the table.

Coefficient of Friction	Speed of Car (cm/s)	Speed of Car (mph)	Skidding Distance (cm)	Skidding Distance (ft)
0.5	1341	30		
0.9	1341	30		
0.5	2012	45		
0.9	2012	45		
0.5	2682	60		
0.9	2682	60		
0.5	4024	90		
0.9	4024	90		

3. In general, what happens to the skidding distance when the speed doubles?
4. Give an example of a situation in which the *smaller* coefficient of friction (0.5) may apply.
5. Give an example of a situation in which the *larger* coefficient of friction (0.9) may apply.
6. Using the length of the skid marks from the crime scene report, calculate the speed of the getaway car, in miles per hour, assuming the smaller coefficient of frictionis correct.
7. Calculate the speed of the car again, in miles per hour, assuming the larger coefficient of friction is correct.
8. Considering the conditions of the road and the getaway car, which coefficient of friction do you think *most likely* applied during the car chase? Explain your answer.
9. Based on your answer to question 8, which suspect's car was *most likely* involved in the car chase?

Case File 13
Life in the Fast Lane: Using skid marks to determine vehicle speed

Teacher Notes

Teaching time: one or two class periods

This lab introduces the coefficient of friction and uses it to determine the speed of a vehicle from the distance of its skid.

Tips

- Preparing the vehicle and computing the coefficient of friction should take about 20 minutes. This depends on how steadily the students pull the vehicle. It may take significantly longer.
- It is important that students zero the force sensor before *each* force measurement because the sensor is affected by very small movements.
- You may want to review balance of forces and Newton's laws of motion with the students before they begin the lab.

Lab Preparation

- If the vehicle you use is fairly lightweight, you may need to add some weight to it to make it slide more stably and in a straighter line.
- Use as smooth a surface as possible (not carpet) to slide the vehicles on. This will enable the students to pull the vehicle with more-constant force and reduce the error in their calculation of μ.

Background Information

If skid marks are present at the scene of an accident, one member of an investigative team is dispatched with a tool, called a trundle wheel, that looks like a walking cane with a small tire on the bottom. This tire is attached to a device similar to a pedometer. It counts the number of times the tire rotates and converts that number into distance traveled, in meters. In this way, the investigator can accurately follow the path of the skid mark and determine its length.

From the length of the skid mark, it is possible to estimate the speed of the vehicle at the start of the skid. This calculation is based on Newton's laws of motion and the formula for the kinetic energy of a moving body. The derivation of the formula is as follows:

$$F_f = \mu mg$$
$$E_k = \tfrac{1}{2}mv^2 = F_f d$$
$$\tfrac{1}{2}mv^2 = (\mu mg)d$$
$$v = \sqrt{2g\mu d}$$

where v is the speed (velocity) at the start of the skid, m is the mass of the vehicle, g is the acceleration due to gravity (9.8 m/sec²), μ is the coefficient of friction, F_f is the force of friction, E_k is kinetic energy, and d is the length of the skid mark.

Notice that, in the final equation, the weight of the vehicle does not appear. Only the speed of the car, the acceleration due to gravity, and the coefficient of friction—which is related to the vehicle's tires and the road's surface—determine the stopping distance.

Modifications

If time permits, you can have the students repeat the experiment on different kinds of surfaces, such as carpet or wood. They could also experiment with different weights in the vehicle. This should help to reinforce the meaning and applications of the coefficient of friction.

Sample Data (using a Hall's Carriage)

	Value
Average Sliding Friction (N) **(Equal to average force used to pull vehicle)**	0.5770
Average weight of vehicle (N)	2.092
Coefficient of friction, μ $\mu = \dfrac{\textit{Sliding friction} \textbf{ (N)}}{\textit{Weight of vehicle} \textbf{ (N)}}$	0.276

Trial Number	Skidding Distance (cm)	Speed (cm/s)
1	15.8	92.5
2	19.2	102
3	22.6	111

Case Analysis Answers

1. Rearrange the speed equation to solve for d, the skidding distance. Show your work.

$$v = \sqrt{2g\mu d}$$
$$v^2 = 2g\mu d$$
$$d = v^2 \div 2g\mu$$

2. In most cases, an accident investigator cannot accurately compute μ, the coefficient of friction. However, tests have been done to establish a range of values for μ that apply to most situations. In general, the coefficient of friction for a car on an asphalt road is between 0.5 and 0.9. Using this information and the equation from question 1, fill in the final two columns in the table.

Coefficient of Friction	Speed of Car (cm/s)	Speed of Car (mph)	Skidding Distance (cm)	Skidding Distance (ft)
0.5	1341	30	1835	60.2
0.9	1341	30	1019	33.4
0.5	2012	45	4131	136
0.9	2012	45	2295	75.3
0.5	2682	60	7340	241
0.9	2682	60	4078	134
0.5	4024	90	16,523	533
0.9	4024	90	9179	301

3. In general, what happens to the skidding distance when the speed doubles?
Stopping distance more than doubles.
4. Give an example of a situation in which the *smaller* coefficient of friction (0.5) may apply.
Situations include wet or icy road, old tires, tires that are incorrectly inflated, and bad brakes.
5. Give an example of a situation in which the *larger* coefficient of friction (0.9) may apply.
Situations include dry road, new and properly inflated tires, and good brakes.
6. Using the length of the skid marks from the crime scene report, calculate the speed of the getaway car, in miles per hour, assuming the smaller coefficient of friction is correct.
105 mph
7. Calculate the speed of the car again, in miles per hour, assuming the larger coefficient of friction is correct.
141 mph
8. Considering the conditions of the road and the getaway car, which coefficient of friction do you think *most likely* applied during the car chase? Explain your answer.
The car was new, so the tires were probably new, but the road was probably wet due to the rain. Answers may vary, but students should clearly support their arguments.
9. Based on your answer to question 8, which suspect's car was *most likely* involved in the car chase?
Answers will vary, depending on the answer to question 8. Given the uncertainty in the coefficient of friction, any one of the three may be the culprit.

Hot Air, Cold Body:
Using Newton's law of cooling to determine time of death

Use Newton's law of cooling to narrow down the number of suspects by determining when the victim was killed.

Memo to Detective Sergeant:

The elevator operator of the Ritz Palace Hotel died from a stab wound while on duty last Thursday evening. His body was discovered by a family on its way down to the pool. When we arrived at the scene, we canvassed the area but found nothing. The elevator is full of fingerprints of the hundreds of guests who ride it during the day. We have several suspects in mind, but we are having trouble pinning down the time of death. If we can determine that, we have a good shot at finding the killer.

Enclosed are a photograph of the crime scene and part of the paramedic report.

Paramedic report

Date: 10/5/05

Time: 9:45 p.m.

Body temperature: 29.0°C

Notes: Elevator temperature was

high; thermostat set at 27°C.

Forensics Objective

- determine the time of death of a person who has died within the last few hours

Science and Mathematics Objectives

- create a temperature vs. time graph for cooling
- use the cooling-rate equation to estimate time of death
- become familiar with Newton's law of cooling

Materials

- TI-83/TI-84 Plus™ Family
- Vernier EasyTemp™ temperature probe
- Vernier EasyData™ application
- ring stand with clamp
- model victim

Procedure

Part I: Collecting the Data · · ·

1. Plug the temperature probe into the USB port on the calculator. The calculator will turn on automatically, and the EasyData App will display the ambient (room) temperature. At the bottom of the screen, just above the menu buttons, the current experimental setup will be displayed.

> **TIP!** At the bottom of the Main screen are five options (⌜File⌝, ⌜Setup⌝, ⌜Start⌝, ⌜Graph⌝, and ⌜Quit⌝). Each of these options can be selected by pressing the calculator key located below it (⟨Y=⟩, ⟨WINDOW⟩, ⟨ZOOM⟩, ⟨TRACE⟩, or ⟨GRAPH⟩).

2. The default experimental setup for the EasyTemp probe is to collect one sample every second for 3 minutes. However, for this experiment, you will need to collect one data point every 10 seconds for 20 minutes. Change the experimental setup so the calculator will collect 120 samples at 10-second intervals for a total experiment time of 1200 seconds.
   a) Select ⌜Setup⌝ from the Main screen.
   b) Select option **2: Time Graph….**
   c) Select ⌜Edit⌝ to change the sample interval.
   d) Press ⟨CLEAR⟩ and then type **10** as the sample interval.
   e) Select ⌜Next⌝ to change the number of samples.
   f) Press ⟨CLEAR⟩ and then type **120** as the number of samples.
   g) Select ⌜Next⌝ to confirm that the experimental setup is correct.
   h) When you have confirmed that the time graph settings are correct (10-second sample interval, 120 samples, 1200-second experiment length), select ⌜OK⌝.

3. Read the ambient (room) temperature from the display on the Main screen and write it in your Evidence Record. Make sure the tip of the probe is not touching anything warmer or cooler than room temperature (such as your hand or the tabletop).

4. Place the tip of the EasyTemp probe into the model victim. Use the ring stand and clamp to hold the probe in place.

5. Select ⌈Start⌉ to begin collecting data. If you get a message about overwriting stored data, select ⌈OK⌉. Data collection will run for 20 minutes. During the data collection, a graph of temperature vs. time will be displayed. When the data collection is complete, the temperature vs. time graph will be scaled and displayed, along with several options for working with the graph. If the screen goes blank during or after the data collection, press ⟨ ON ⟩ to restore it.

6. When data collection is complete, use the arrow keys to "trace" your temperature vs. time graph. The cursor will move along the curve. The x-value (time in seconds) will be displayed at the top of the screen next to **X=**. The y-value (temperature in degrees Celsius) will be displayed next to **Y=**.
    a) Trace the graph to locate the maximum temperature reached by the model victim during the data collection. Record this temperature as the initial temperature of the model in your Evidence Record. (Note: The maximum temperature will probably *not* be the first temperature reading on your graph; be sure to trace the graph to find the *maximum* temperature).
    b) In your Evidence Record, write the time (in seconds) at which the maximum temperature occurred. This is the initial time.
    c) Locate the minimum temperature reached by the model, and record it in your Evidence Record as the final temperature. Record the time it occurred as the time of minimum model temperature. This is the final time. (Note: The minimum temperature should be the *last* point on your graph).
    d) Subtract the initial time from the final time to find how long your model victim was cooling. Enter this time in your Evidence Record as the duration of model temperature measurement.

7. Before removing the temperature probe, exit the EasyData App.
    a) Select ⌈Main⌉ to return to the Main screen.
    b) Select ⌈Quit⌉ then ⌈OK⌉ to return to the Home screen.
    c) You can now remove the temperature probe.

Part II: Analyzing the Data ⦿ ⦿ ⦿

To use your data to determine time of death, you can use Newton's law of cooling:

$$\text{cooling time} = \left(\frac{1}{k}\right)\ln\left(\frac{\text{initial temperature} - \text{ambient temperature}}{\text{final temperature} - \text{ambient temperature}}\right)$$

where *k* is the cooling constant. You can use your calculator to solve this equation for different variables. First you will solve the equation for *k*. Then you will use this value of *k* to determine an estimate for how long the body was cooling before its temperature was measured.

8. First, enter the equation for Newton's law of cooling into your calculator's equation solver.
    a) From the Home screen, press ⟨MATH⟩. Select option **0: Solver...**. You should see a screen that looks like this:

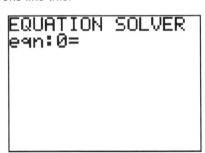

```
EQUATION SOLVER
eqn:0=
```

If the **eqn:0=** line is not blank, use the ⟨▲⟩ key to move to the **eqn:0=** line and press ⟨CLEAR⟩ to clear it.

b) In order for the calculator to solve the equation for you, the left side of the equation must be equal to 0. To rewrite the Newton's law of cooling equation so that the left side is 0, subtract "cooling time" from both sides of the equation. This will leave you with the following equation:

$$0 = \left(\frac{1}{k}\right) \ln\left(\frac{\text{initial temperature} - \text{ambient temperature}}{\text{final temperature} - \text{ambient temperature}}\right) - \text{cooling time}$$

c) You will need to use letters to represent each variable in the equation. Use **K** for *k*, **I** for initial temperature, **A** for ambient temperature, **F** for final temperature, and **T** for cooling time. With these letters substituted for the different variables, the equation looks like this:

$$0 = \left(\frac{1}{K}\right) \ln\left(\frac{I - A}{F - A}\right) - T$$

d) You will need to type the Newton's law of cooling equation into the equation solver. Remember that you can type letters onto the screen by pressing (ALPHA) and then pressing the calculator key that has the letter you want written above it in green. For example, the letter **K** is inserted by pressing (ALPHA) (( ), and the letter **T** is inserted by pressing (ALPHA) (4).

e) Now begin entering the equation into the calculator. Type (( ) (1) (÷) (ALPHA) (( ) ( )) to insert **(1/K)**. This inserts the first part of the Newton's law of cooling equation. Do *not* press (ENTER).

f) Type (x) (LN) to enter the natural logarithm, ln, function. Do *not* press (ENTER). Notice that a left parenthesis is automatically inserted when you insert the natural log function. You will have to close the parentheses when you are finished entering the equation.

g) Press (( ) (ALPHA) (x²) (–) (ALPHA) (MATH) ( )) to enter the numerator of the equation inside the natural logarithm. Do *not* press (ENTER).

h) Type (÷) (( ) (ALPHA) (COS) (–) (ALPHA) (MATH) ( )) ( )) to enter the denominator and close the parentheses around the natural logarithm. Do *not* press (ENTER).

i) Type (–) (ALPHA) (4) to enter **-T**. Your screen should now look like this:

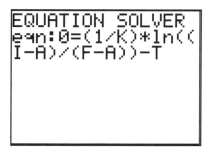

Notice that the equation you have just entered looks like the equation from step 8c.

j) Press (ENTER). Your screen should give the equation and then a list of the five variables: **K**, **I**, **A**, **F**, and **T**. The screen should look like this:

```
(1/K)*ln((I-A...=0
K=0
I=0
A=0
F=0
T=0
bound={-1E99,1...
```

(Note: Don't worry if the values next to the variables are different from those in the screen shot. You're going to change them in the next step anyway.)

9. Now use the solver function to calculate the value of *k*, the cooling constant.

> If you make a mistake or if there are already values assigned to the variables, use the arrow keys to move to the variable and then type in the correct value.

a) In order for the calculator to solve for *k*, you need to give it a starting "guess" for the value. In most cases, *k* is approximately 0.0001. Enter **0.0001** for the **K** variable. Press ⟨ENTER⟩ to move to the next variable.

b) Recall that variable **I** stands for the initial temperature of the object that is cooling. For variable **I**, type in the initial temperature for the model that you measured. This is the *maximum* temperature that you recorded from your temperature graph in step 6. Press ⟨ENTER⟩ to move to the next variable. (Note: Type in *only* the number values for your temperatures. Do not type in °, C, or any other symbols. For 23°C, simply type in **23**.)

c) Variable **A** stands for the ambient (room) temperature around the object that is cooling. For variable **A**, type in the ambient air temperature that you recorded in step 3. Press ⟨ENTER⟩ to move to the next variable.

d) For variable **F** (the final temperature of the cooling object), type in the final (minimum) temperature of the model. Press ⟨ENTER⟩ to move to the next variable.

e) For variable **T** (the cooling time), type in the duration of the model temperature measurement (in seconds) that you calculated in step 6d (it should be no longer than 1200 seconds).

f) The calculator will solve the equation for whichever variable is highlighted. Since you want to solve for *k*, use the arrow keys to move the cursor to highlight the number next to **K**. Do *not* press ⟨ENTER⟩.

g) Press ⟨ALPHA⟩ ⟨ENTER⟩ to select the **SOLVE** function and solve the equation for **K**. (Note: It may take a few seconds for the calculator to solve for **K**. Be patient!) The **K** value will probably be a very long decimal number followed by .... In order to see the value of this number more clearly, go back to the Home screen by pressing ⟨2nd⟩ ⟨MODE⟩. Type **K** by pressing ⟨ALPHA⟩ ⟨(⟩. Then press ⟨ENTER⟩ to display the value of **K**. For example, in the sample screen below, **K** is equal to 2.20 × 10⁻⁴.

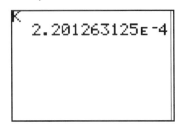

h) Write the value of *k* in your Evidence Record. Record three significant figures.

10. Now that you know the cooling constant, you can use the solver function to determine how long the body cooled before the paramedics measured its temperature. To figure this out, you need to solve the cooling equation for **T**, cooling time.

a) Press ⟨MATH⟩ ⟨0⟩ to go back to the equation solver screen.

b) Leave the **K** variable set to its current value. Press ⟨ENTER⟩ to move to the **I** variable. In this case, the body cooled from normal body temperature (37°C) to its temperature when it was measured. The initial temperature was therefore 37°C. Record this in the Evidence Record, then type **37** for **I** in the calculator and press ⟨ENTER⟩ to move to the next variable.

c) The ambient temperature, **A**, should be set to the temperature of the elevator the body was found in. Check the evidence report to find this temperature. Write it in the Evidence Record and then enter it into variable **A**. Press ⟨ENTER⟩ to move to the next variable.

d) The final temperature, **F**, is the temperature of the body when it was measured by the paramedics. Check the evidence report for this temperature, record it in your Evidence Record, and then type it into the space for the **F** variable. Press ⟨ENTER⟩ to move to the next variable.

e) In this case, you are trying to solve for **T**, which is the length of time the body was cooling before the paramedics measured its temperature. Press ⬭CLEAR⬭ to clear the value of **T**, and enter a "guess" of 1800 seconds for the cooling time. (The body was probably in the elevator for longer than 1800 seconds, which is about half an hour, but the guess you give the calculator does not have to be completely accurate).

f) Leave the cursor on the **T** variable and press ⬭ALPHA⬭ ⬭ENTER⬭ to solve the equation for **T**.

g) Record the value of *t* in seconds in your Evidence Record.

h) Convert the cooling time from seconds to minutes by dividing it by 60. Write the cooling time in minutes in your Evidence Record.

11. To determine time of death, subtract the number of minutes that the body was cooling from the time that the temperature was measured. Enter the time of death into the Evidence Record.

Name: _____

Date: _____

Evidence Record

From the Model
Ambient (room) temperature for model (°C) _____

Initial temperature of model (°C) _____

Final temperature of model (°C) _____

Time of maximum model temperature (s) _____

Time of minimum model temperature (s) _____

Duration of model temperature measurement (s) _____

Cooling constant, k _____

From the Evidence Report
Ambient (room) temperature for body (°C) _____

Time body temperature was measured _____

Temperature of body (°C) _____

Cooling time, t (s) _____

Cooling time, t (min) _____

Actual time of death _____

Case Report

Prepare a report stating the conclusions of your investigation. In your report, be sure to include the temperature measurements that you made, all of your calculations, and the estimated time of death you calculated. How accurate do you think your time-of-death estimate is? What factors can exist that may make your time-of-death estimate inaccurate? What factors can exist that may make a *real* time-of-death estimate inaccurate?

Case File 14
Hot Air, Cold Body:
Using Newton's law of cooling to determine time of death

Teacher Notes

Teaching time: one class period

This lab introduces a practical use for Newton's law of cooling and the equation that describes it.

Tips

- You'll need to practice the lab to find out what the cooling rates are like in your room.
- There will be approximately 20 minutes during which the calculator will be collecting temperature data but the students will not actively be doing anything. This may be a good time to review Newton's law of cooling or explain some background information.
- If you wish, you can have each group's model "victim" start at a different body temperature by heating the canisters in water baths of different temperatures.

Lab Preparation

Materials for making the model victim
- sodium polyacrylate (water lock; can be purchased through chemical supply companies)
- Gatorade® or water
- 35 mm film canister, with hole in lid the size of temperature probe tip

Instructions for making the model victim
1. Place 1 g sodium polyacrylate in an empty film canister.
2. Fill the canister three-fourths full of Gatorade or water.
3. Put the cap on the canister and shake it gently, making sure to cover the hole.
4. Warm the canister in your hands. Alternatively, you can place the canister in a water bath set to the desired temperature.

Background Information

Body temperature readings for actual time-of-death estimates are usually taken rectally or intra-abdominally (in the liver). Ear, mouth, or armpit temperatures are generally considered inaccurate for these measurements. Depending on the level of your students, you may or may not wish to mention this or explore it further. In real life, the rate of cooling depends upon many things. The size of the body, how the body is dressed, the room temperature, where the corpse is located, and humidity all affect how fast a corpse cools. For this reason, investigators often use several different methods to estimate time of death. You should emphasize to your students that the model they are using to determine the cooling constant is just that—*a model*.

Resources

http://www.dundee.ac.uk/forensicmedicine/llb/timedeath.htm
This site from the University of Dundee (UK) includes interesting quotations on the difficulties in determining time of death, as well as a thorough exploration of the many changes that occur in the body after death.

http://www.pathguy.com/TimeDead.htm
This site contains a Java-based interactive time-of-death calculator. It also includes links to several other good forensic pathology sources.

Modifications

- You can ask more-advanced students to investigate other methods of determining time of death (e.g., forensic entomology). However, be aware that many resources and methods may involve rather gruesome pictures, descriptions, or diagrams. You can also introduce and discuss some of the major sources of error in estimating time of death from body temperature. For example, what would happen to the time-of-death estimate if the person had a fever when he or she died? What if the person died of hypothermia?
- Students who are less comfortable or experienced using the calculator can solve the cooling-rate equation by hand, without using the calculator's equation solver function. To do this, use the following information and steps for Procedure Part II:

To use your data to determine time of death, you can use Newton's law of cooling, as follows:

$$\text{cooling time} = \left(\frac{1}{k}\right)\ln\left(\frac{\text{initial temperature} - \text{ambient temperature}}{\text{final temperature} - \text{ambient temperature}}\right)$$

where k is the cooling constant. First, you will rearrange the equation to solve for k for the temperature measurements that you took with the model. Then, you will solve for cooling time, using the equation and the measurements that the paramedics took of the victim. Once you know how long the body was cooling before it was measured by the paramedics, you can figure out what time the victim died.

8. In order to solve for k, you need to rearrange the Newton's law of cooling equation as follows:

$$k = \frac{1}{\text{cooling time}}\ln\left(\frac{\text{initial temperature of model} - \text{ambient temperature}}{\text{final temperature of model} - \text{ambient temperature}}\right)$$

Using the values for time and temperature that you measured for the model, solve the equation above to determine the value of k. Record this value in your Evidence Record.

9. Now you can use the Newton's law of cooling equation to solve for the cooling time.

$$\text{cooling time} = \frac{1}{k}\ln\left(\frac{\text{normal body temperature (37°C)} - \text{ambient temperature}}{\text{temperature of body when found} - \text{ambient temperature}}\right)$$

a) Look at the evidence report to learn the temperature of the body when it was measured and the ambient temperature of the elevator. Write these values in your Evidence Record.

b) Solve the equation above for cooling time, using the value of k that you calculated in step 8 and the temperatures you just recorded from the evidence report. The cooling time that you get will be in seconds. Record the cooling time in seconds in your Evidence Record.

c) Convert the cooling time from seconds to minutes by dividing it by 60. Record the cooling time in minutes in your Evidence Record.

10. To determine the time of death, subtract the number of minutes that the body was cooling from the time it was measured. Record the time of death in your Evidence Record.

Sample Data (using Gatorade)

From the Model

Ambient (room) temperature for model (°C)	23.0°C
Initial temperature of model (°C)	28.6°C
Final temperature of model (°C)	27.3°C
Time of maximum model temperature (s)	0 s
Time of minimum model temperature (s)	1200 s
Duration of model temperature measurement (s)	1200 s
Cooling constant, k	2.20×10^{-4}

From the Evidence Record

Ambient (room) temperature for body (°C)	27°C
Time body temperature was measured	9:45 p.m.
Temperature of body (°C)	29.0°C
Cooling time, t (s)	7311 s
Cooling time, t (min)	122 min
Actual time of death	7:43 p.m.

Case Report Notes

In their case reports, students should indicate understanding of the various factors that could have affected their calculations. For example, the cooling constant for the model was probably not the same as the cooling constant for the body. In addition, temperature or time measurements could have been inaccurate (due to mistakes in reading the graph or to sampling frequency). The students should also indicate an understanding that many factors influence a real time-of-death estimate. These factors include the size and composition of the body, how the body is dressed, humidity, location of the body, whether the body has been touching anything very hot or cold, the person's body temperature before death, whether the body was moved, whether the ambient temperature was constant, and whether body temperature equaled ambient temperature.

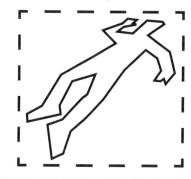

Appendix A:
Calculator Basics for the TI-84 Plus™ Family

More-extensive directions for using the TI-84 Plus family of calculators can be found in the user manual or online at http://education.ti.com.

Note: Unless the directions specifically say otherwise, "press the ___ button" means to press the button once and release it before pressing the next button.

Turning the Calculator On and Off ● ● ●

- To turn the calculator on, press the ⟨ON⟩ button in the lower left corner.
- To turn the calculator off, press the ⟨2nd⟩ button (blue button in the upper left corner) and then the ⟨ON⟩ button.
- The calculator has an "auto-off" function that shuts it down automatically, to conserve battery power, if you do not push any buttons for 5 minutes. If your screen goes blank, you can restore it by pressing ⟨ON⟩.
- When the calculator shuts off (either automatically or because you have pressed ⟨2nd⟩ ⟨ON⟩, all information on the screen and in the memory is automatically saved. This means that, if the calculator shuts off during an experiment, you simply have to press ⟨ON⟩ and all of your calculations will be visible again. You won't lose any data.

Understanding the Directions in This Book ● ● ●

- The procedures for each lab contain some images to help you follow the directions. When you need to press a certain button on your calculator, the text shows a small image of that button. For example, if you need to press the ENTER key, the text shows an image like this: ⟨ENTER⟩.
- Many of the procedures require that you select menu items from the calculator display. These menu items appear in two forms: as "tabs" and as "lists." A "tab" menu item appears on the bottom of the screen inside a small box. To select one of these items, push the button that is directly below the tab. In this book, "tab" menu items are shown as small images like this: ⟨Setup⟩.
- "List" menu items appear on the screen in the form of a list. They are usually numbered. To select a numbered list item, press the appropriate number button on the calculator. To select a list item that is not numbered, use the arrow keys to highlight the item, and then press ⟨ENTER⟩. In this book, menu items are shown in a different font, like this: **2: Time Graph**.

The Arrow Keys, the Cursor, and Highlighting ● ● ●

- The cursor is the blinking box that appears on your calculator screen. It shows you where your next entry will appear on the screen.
- The arrow keys are located in the upper right corner of your calculator keypad. They can be used to move the cursor around the screen.
- Many of the procedures in this book ask you to highlight certain options on the screen. Some options blink when they are highlighted. Other options are printed in reverse color (light writing on a dark background).

Using the ⟨2nd⟩ *and* ⟨ALPHA⟩ *Buttons* ● ● ●

- Most of the buttons on the calculator have more than one function. For example, the ⟨ON⟩ button can be used to turn the calculator off also. The second (and third, if any) functions of the buttons can be accessed by pressing the ⟨2nd⟩ and ⟨ALPHA⟩ keys.
- To access a function written in blue above one of the calculator buttons, press the ⟨2nd⟩ key and then the button with the desired function above it. For example, to use the square root function, press ⟨2nd⟩ and then ⟨x^2⟩. When you press the ⟨2nd⟩ button, the cursor changes from a box to a blinking ↑.

- To access a function written in green above one of the calculator buttons, press the ⬭ALPHA⬭ key and then the button with the desired function above it. Most of the ⬭ALPHA⬭ key functions are letters. You can use these letters to name variables, write programs, and assign functions. For example, to write D to your calculator screen, press ⬭ALPHA⬭ ⬭x⁻¹⬭. When you press the ⬭ALPHA⬭ button, the cursor changes to a blinking **A**.

The Home and Main Screens ● ● ●

- The Home screen is the screen where you can enter expressions, numbers, and symbols. Most of the time, the screen that you see when you first turn on the calculator is the Home screen. The Home screen may be blank or it may show the last few calculations that you performed. In most cases, selecting **QUIT** by pressing ⬭2nd⬭ ⬭MODE⬭ will return you to the Home screen.
- If you connect a probe or sensor to your calculator's USB port when the calculator is turned off, it will automatically turn on and show you the probe or sensor's Main screen. This screen shows you the options you have for controlling the input to and output from the probe or sensor. In most cases, selecting ⌐Main⌐, ⌐Cancl⌐, or ⌐OK⌐ will return you to the Main screen.

A Few More Important Points ● ● ●

- The TI calculators have different buttons for the negative sign and the minus sign. The ⬭−⬭ key inserts a minus sign. Use this key when you are subtracting two numbers (for example, to enter the expression 35 - 23). The ⬭(-)⬭ key inserts a negative sign. Use this key when you are inserting a negative number (for example, when entering the exponent part of 3.2×10^{-2}).
- Be sure to use parentheses (⬭(⬭ and ⬭)⬭) when you write complicated expressions. This helps ensure that the operations are carried out in the correct order.
- The TI graphing calculators use the E symbol for scientific notation. For example, the number 2.355×10^5 will display as 2.355E5.
- To type in a number in scientific notation, use ⬭2nd⬭ ⬭,⬭ to insert the E notation. For example, to enter the number 1.55×10^{-3}, first type 1.55, then press ⬭2nd⬭ ⬭,⬭ to insert the E , then type -3 (don't forget to use the ⬭(-)⬭ button, not the ⬭−⬭ button, to insert the negative sign).

Note:
The activities contained in this book are written for use with the Vernier EasyData™ App for the TI-84 Plus™, Vernier EasyTemp™, Vernier EasyLink™, and the CBR 2™. You may also use the CBL 2™ or Vernier LabPro® data collection devices with the EasyData App for TI-83 Plus or TI-84 Plus calculators. The only difference between the written instructions in the book and the use of the forensics activities with CBL 2 or LabPro is that you will need to launch the EasyData App from the Apps menu of the calculator.

Appendix B:
EasyData Reference

In this book, you use the TI-83 Plus or TI-84 Plus graphing calculators connected to a data collection device to collect, examine, analyze, and graph data in the activities. Once Vernier EasyData™ is installed on your calculator, it can be accessed by pressing the APPS key.

How Do I Get EasyData on My Calculator

EasyData is part of the bundle of Apps that come preloaded on all new TI-84 Plus and TI-84 PlusSilver Edition graphing calculators manufactured after January 2005. To check to see if EasyData is on your calculator, press APPS and scroll through the list of loaded applications. If your graphing calculator does not contain the EasyData App, you can download EasyData from the Vernier Web site: www.vernier.com/easy.html. Then use TI Connect to transfer it to your graphing calculator.

Using TI Connect™ to Load EasyData

TI Connect software is a universal application that is compatible with many calculators..

Windows Computers Running Windows 98, NT 4.x, 2000 or ME, and XP

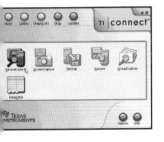

1. Connect the TI-GRAPH LINK cable, or the TI Connectivity cable, to the serial or USB port of your computer and to the port at the bottom edge of the TI-83 Plus graphing calculator.

   Note: If you are using the TI-84 Plus or TI-84 Plus Silver Edition, connect the TI USB cable to the USB port of your computer and to the USB port at the top edge of your graphing calculator.

2. Start the TI Connect software on your computer. Click on Device Explorer.

3. The program will identify the attached device and call up a window representing the contents.

4. Loading programs and applications onto a TI graphing calculator is very easy. All you have to do is drag the program or application from wherever you have it on your computer to the Device Explorer window, and it will copy onto your graphing calculator.

5. The program should now be loaded into your calculator. To confirm this, press APPS on the calculator to display the loaded applications.

Macintosh Computers Running Mac® OS X 10.2 (Jaguar), 10.3 (Panther), and 10.4 (Tiger)

1. Connect the TI-GRAPH LINK cable, or the TI Connectivity cable, to the USB port of your computer and to the port at the bottom edge of the TI-83 Plus or TI-83 Plus Silver Edition graphing calculator.

   Note: If you are using the TI-84 Plus or TI-84 Plus Silver Edition graphing calculator, connect the TI USB cable to the USB port of your computer and to the USB port at the top edge of your graphing calculator.

2. Turn the calculator on. On the computer, start TI Device Explorer.

3. The program will identify the attached device and call up a window representing the contents.

4. Loading programs onto a TI graphing calculator is very easy. All you have to do is drag the program to the device's window, and it will copy onto your graphing calculator.

5. The program should now be loaded into your calculator. To confirm this, press ⟨APPS⟩ on the calculator to display the loaded applications.

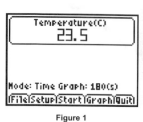

Figure 1

Main Screen

The Main screen of EasyData is shown in Figure 1. The top portion of the screen displays the sensor currently in use—in this case a temperature probe. A sensor reading is also displayed. The lower portion of the screen displays the default data collection mode for the sensor. Five options are listed across the bottom of the screen, which correspond to the five calculator keys directly below them. The Main screen of EasyData can be used as a meter; the sensor readings are updated approximately every second.

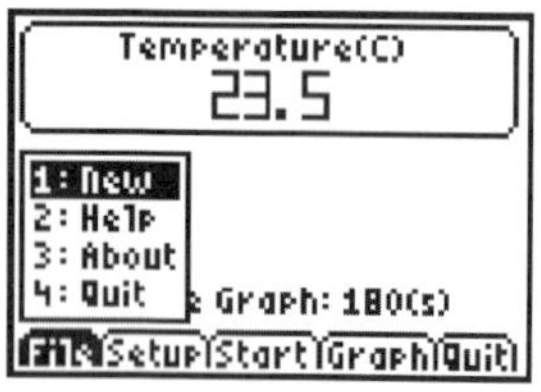

File Menu

The File menu contains four options. When you select File by pressing the ⟨Y=⟩ key, a pop-up menu appears, as shown in Figure 2. When you select the first option, **New**, the EasyData program is reset, and it will return to the Main screen. You should select **New** at the beginning of an experiment as a matter of routine or when you want to confirm that the program has all of the default values in place for the sensor and the data collection. Select **Help** to view the four screens of the help tips for EasyData. Select **About** to see the splash screen, which tells you which version of EasyData you are running and the firmware version of any connected interface. After a moment, the program will return to the Main screen. Select **Quit** to exit EasyData.

Figure 2

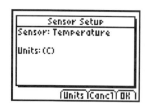

Figure 3

Setup Menu

The Setup menu lists options for the sensors in use and the data collection mode and for zeroing a sensor. Shown in Figure 3 is the Setup menu when a temperature probe is used. Please see the section below for more information about the Setup menu.

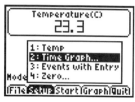

Figure 4

Start, Graph, and Quit Options

Select ⟨Start⟩ to begin data collection. Select ⟨Graph⟩ to view a graph of data that you have already collected. Select ⟨Quit⟩ to exit the EasyData application.

Using the Setup Menu

The Setup menu offers a list of options that depends on the sensor (s) being used. Figure 4 shows the Main screen of EasyData when ⟨Setup⟩ is selected. The sensor in use is displayed at the top of the list, followed by the data collection options. The last item listed is **Zero...**, the option to zero a sensor. The following example shows you how to use the Setup menu with a temperature probe.

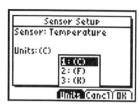

Figure 5

1: TEMP

When you select **1:TEMP**, the sensor setup screen is displayed (Figure 5). This screen identifies the sensor and the units of measure. There are three options displayed at the bottom of the screen: ⟨Units⟩, ⟨Cancl⟩, and ⟨OK⟩.

When you select ⟨Cancl⟩ or ⟨OK⟩, you are sent back to the Main screen.

Figure 6

When you select ⟨Units⟩, you can view the units of measure that are available for use with the sensor. For example, when using a temperature probe, you may choose to display and record the temperature readings in degrees Celsius, degrees Fahrenheit, or the kelvin absolute temperature scale (Figure 6). (Kelvin temperature values are not referred to as "degrees," nor is the degree symbol used.)

2: Time Graph...

When you select the time graph option, the time graph default settings for your sensor are displayed (Figure 7). Please note that these are the default values for the auto-ID sensor being used with EasyData. There are three options displayed at the bottom of the screen: ⟨Edit⟩, ⟨Cancl⟩, and ⟨OK⟩.

When you select ⟨Cancl⟩ or ⟨OK⟩, you are sent back to the Main screen.

Figure 7

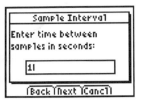

Figure 8

Figure 9

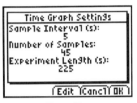

Figure 10

Figure 11

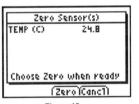

Figure 12

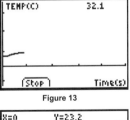

Figure 13

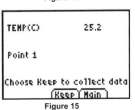

Figure 15

Select ⌈Edit⌉ to change the time graph settings. The first screen to appear is the sample interval screen (Figure 8). It displays the current data collection interval, in seconds, with the cursor next to the value. You can delete the current value by pressing ⟨CLEAR⟩ or by pressing ⟨◁⟩ and ⟨DEL⟩. You can also type over the current value by pressing ⟨◁⟩ and entering a new sample interval. Note that EasyData allows only certain sample intervals. If you enter a sample interval that EasyData does not support, an error message will appear and a sample interval will be chosen for you.

If, at any time, you wish to stop what you are doing and return to the Main screen, select ⌈Cancl⌉. The original values will be restored.

When you have entered a new sample interval or decided to use the default interval, you can continue by selecting ⌈Next⌉. A new screen entitled "Number of Samples" will appear (Figure 9). It displays the default value. You may delete and enter numbers in this screen as you did with the sample interval screen. Again, note that EasyData allows a maximum number of samples based on the sensor in use.

When you have made the desired changes, select ⌈Next⌉. The new time graph settings will be displayed (Figure 10). EasyData always expresses time in seconds; it cannot be changed to minutes or hours. If you select ⌈Cancl⌉ from this screen, the original settings will be restored and you will go to the Main screen. If you select ⌈Edit⌉, you will go back to the sample interval screen. Select ⌈OK⌉ to accept the new time graph settings and return to the Main screen.

3: Events with Entry…
When you select the Events with Entry option, you are changing the data collection mode to one that is independent of time. There are no other choices to be made, thus after you select **Events with Entry...**, the screen goes blank for a second or two and then returns to the Main screen. The new mode is displayed at the bottom of the screen (Figure 11).

4: Zero…
Select this option when you wish to set the current sensor reading to zero. Allow the sensor readings to stabilize, and then select ⌈Zero⌉ (Figure 12).

Data Collection

Time Graph
In most instances, data are plotted as they are collected (Figure 13). This is known as live data collection. If the data collection rate is too fast or too slow, the data collection will be non-live and "Sampling" will appear on the screen until data collection has finished.

To collect data, select ⌈Start⌉ from the Main screen. During live data collection the screen will change to a graph and the data will be plotted. The data collection will cease automatically, according to the sampling parameters. However, you can halt the data collection early by selecting ⌈Stop⌉. After the data collection ends, the graph autoscales to best fit the data. The calculator vernacular for this process is "ZoomStat." Figure 14 shows the autoscaled version of the previous graph. Press ⟨▷⟩ or ⟨◁⟩ to trace the data and examine individual data pairs which are displayed at the top of the graph. Select [Main] to return to the Main screen.

Events with Entry
Select ⌈Start⌉ from the Main screen to begin data collection. The screen will change to display a sensor reading and list the data point that you will be collecting (Figure 15). When the reading has stabilized, select ⌈Keep⌉ to collect the data point.

The "Enter Value" dialog box will appear (Figure 16). The cursor will rest in a box beneath the title.

Type the value for the independent variable (*x*-value), and then select ⌈OK⌉. Repeat this process to collect subsequent data points.

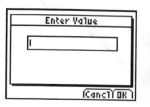

Figure 16

After you have collected two data points, the screen will display a graph of your data. The current sensor reading will appear at the top of the screen, and you will have two options from this point on. Select ⌈**Keep**⌉ to collect a data point, or select ⌈**Stop**⌉ to halt the data collection and see an autoscaled graph of your data.

Using the Sample Data Files

The CD inside the back cover of this book includes sample data files for each calculator for each activity. The sample data let you evaluate the activity without setting up and performing the activity procedures. To use the sample data, use TI Connect to drag the sample data files onto your graphing calculator. Once the sample data files have been loaded, proceed to the Analysis section of the activity and follow the instructions for working with the data.

Appendix C:
What You'll Need to Complete All Activities in This Book

What You'll Need to Complete All Activities in This Book

Calculators, Applications, and Sensors
- TI83/TI-84 Plus™ Family
- Calculator-Based Laboratory 2™ (CBL 2 ™) and link cables
- Calculator-Based Ranger 2™ (CBR 2™)
- Colorimeters
- cuvettes for Colorimeters
- Conductivity Probes
- Dual-Range Force Sensors
- pH Sensors
- Vernier EasyData™ application
- Vernier EasyLink™
- Vernier EasyTemp™ temperature probes
- Vernier Microphones

Chemicals
- acetone
- baby formula, powdered (optional)
- baking powder (optional)
- baking soda (optional)
- clay or mud (optional)
- corn starch (optional)
- deionized or distilled water
- Epsom salts (optional)
- flour (optional)
- Gatorade® (optional)
- ground chalk (optional)
- HCl aqueous solution, 1 M (optional)
- ink samples from different types of pens
- isopropanol
- lime (optional)
- methanol
- NaCl aqueous solution, 1 M (optional)
- NaOH aqueous solution, 1 M (optional)
- plaster of paris (optional)
- powdered sugar (optional)
- simulated blood
- sodium polyacrylate
- talcum powder (optional)
- *tert*-butyl alcohol
- topsoil or soil taken from different locations
- vinegar

Glassware and Lab Ware
- balances
- beakers, 250 mL
- beakers, 400 mL
- beakers, 50 mL
- beakers, waste
- calipers, or compass and metric ruler
- colored wax pencils
- dropper bottles
- filter papers, coarse, 12.5 cm diameter
- funnels, medium

- goggles
- graduated cylinders, 100 mL
- Hall's carriages or heavy toy cars
- lint-free tissues
- magnifying glasses or hand lenses
- metric rulers
- metric tape measures or metersticks
- pipettes or droppers, disposable
- pipettes or graduated cylinders, 10 mL
- ring stands with clamps
- soft tuning-fork hammers
- spoons or weighing papers
- stirring rods
- test-tube racks
- test tubes
- tuning forks of 6 different frequencies
- wash bottles with distilled or deionized water

Other Materials
- 35 mm film canisters
- blocks of wood (optional)
- books, 2 cm thick
- books, 5–7 cm thick
- boxes, large
- boxes, small (optional)
- C-clamp or heavy tape
- masking tape
- mug (optional)
- newspapers
- peat moss (optional)
- pennies dated 1963–1981
- pennies dated 1982 (optional)
- pennies dated after 1982
- ramp made from strong cardboard or wood, 1.5 m × 25 cm
- red food coloring
- roll of tape (optional)
- rubber bands, small
- rubber bands, wide (optional)
- sand (optional)
- staplers (optional)
- straight walkway at least 10 m long
- thread, string, or yarn
- toy cars, at least 5 cm tall
- vehicles, about 7 cm tall with mass of 450–500 g
- white paper